Science
through
Children's Literature

SCIENCE THROUGH CHILDREN'S LITERATURE
An Integrated Approach

Carol M. Butzow
Educational Consultant

and

John W. Butzow
Dean, College of Education
Indiana University of Pennsylvania

Illustrated by
Hannah L. Ben-Zvi

1989
TEACHER IDEAS PRESS
A Division of
Libraries Unlimited, Inc.
Englewood, Colorado

TEACHER IDEAS PRESS
A Division of Libraries Unlimited, Inc.
P.O. Box 3988
Englewood, Colorado 80155-3988

Library of Congress Cataloging-in-Publication Data

Butzow, Carol M., 1942-
    Science through children's literature : an integrated approach /
Carol M. Butzow and John W. Butzow ; illustrated by Hannah L. Ben
-Zvi.
    xviii, 240 p. 22x28 cm.
    Includes bibliographical references.
    ISBN 0-87287-667-5
    1. Science--Study and teaching (Elementary)   2. Activity programs
in education.   3. Children--Books and reading.   I. Butzow, John W.
II. Title.
LB1585.B85   1989
372.3'5044--dc20   89-20152
                                                              CIP

To our daughters, Karen and Kristen

CONTENTS

PART I
USING CHILDREN'S LITERATURE
AS A SPRINGBOARD TO SCIENCE

PART III
EARTH AND SPACE SCIENCE

PART IV
PHYSICAL SCIENCE

ACKNOWLEDGMENTS

To our parents, for their encouragement and support, especially Eunice Hollander who read many manuscripts and took over many of our responsibilities so we could work on this project.

To our friends, especially Mary Schmidt, for sharing their ideas on books and activities and how they can be integrated into the classroom experience.

To Charles Mack, Elaine Davis, and the third grade students of United Elementary School, Armagh, Pennsylvania, for allowing Carol the pleasure of teaching *Mike Mulligan and His Steam Shovel* as an integrated unit.

To the many teachers who have attended our workshops, conference presentations, and classes, for accepting and implementing our ideas and encouraging us to compile them into a book.

To Susan Sewell and Scott Palermo of the Delaware Valley Middle School, Milford, Pennsylvania, for sharing bibliographies and ideas about our mutual interests of science and children's literature.

To Nancy Nicholls of the Bangor Public Library, Bangor, Maine, and Jean Blake of the University of Maine Library, Orono, Maine, for their assistance in locating books and bibliographies during the initial phase of this work.

To the workers of the Pinocchio Bookstore, Pittsburgh, Pennsylvania, for recommending and obtaining many of the books we used in our work.

To the Northern New England Marine Education Project, University of Maine, for permission to adapt the illustrations related to ocean life.

To the graphics staff of the Media Resources Department, Indiana University of Pennsylvania (IUP) Library, for designing the concept maps included in this book.

To Paul Kornfeld, for analyzing and evaluating our proposed illustration list.

To Michael T. Pierce, for help in locating musical references.

Especially, to Kathleen Gaylor and the student workers of the IUP College of Education Dean's office, for their assistance in the preparation of this manuscript.

INTRODUCTION

At the present time, parallel events are occurring in the fields of reading instruction and science instruction. Reading is no longer seen as the end product of decoding words. Nor is it a hierarchy of isolated subskills which, when "mastered," lead automatically to comprehension. Instead, reading is the interaction of the reader's experiential background and knowledge (schema) with the author's background and purpose, and with the text itself. Comprehension is actively constructed by the reader as these three elements interact. Skills are interdependent and cannot exist alone. No single process can be performed without overlapping others. When viewed from this perspective, it is necessary to process only three basic skills to become proficient readers—word knowledge, reasoning, and relationships (Spache and Spache, 1986).

In science, the memorization of facts and vocabulary words is somewhat akin to working with skills in isolation in the reading class. It is an experience that lends itself to mental activity, but it does not necessarily provide an increase in knowledge or facilitate the ability to reason and see relationships. While it is necessary to acquire factual knowledge, it is more important that children understand the conceptual framework that relates these facts one to the other and to the world in which the children live. Since the amount of knowledge upon which we draw is doubling every few years, reliance on factual memory is insufficient for producing students who will understand the role and use of science in a technological world. Science is a product to acquire facts, principles, theories and laws; a process or method to investigate problems, make hypotheses, evaluate data; and an attitude acquainted with science values, opinions, and beliefs.

Both science and reading are processes that must be partially constructed by the learner, by combining the child's preknowledge with new information. Children must experience learning and be allowed to build meanings and relationships for themselves. Only then will they have learned to read, not decode, and to understand concepts, not memorize.

The purpose of this book is to suggest an alternative approach to the teaching of elementary science in light of more contemporary definitions of both reading and science. This method utilizes well-selected and conceptually and factually correct works of fictional children's literature. Although the method is most easily applied with picture books aimed at grades K-3, it is also possible to employ it in higher grades using shorter "chapter books" or by excerpting longer sources. Although fiction books can be used to motivate students and to provide background for the science class, as suggested by Dole and Johnson (1981) or Guerra and Payne (1981), this is not their only function. Nor are fiction works a means of clarifying concepts that may then be presented by other methods (Smardo, 1982); they can be the actual factual and conceptual basis of a science lesson.

Part I of this book presents an integrated approach to scientific instruction using children's fictional literature as its foundation. It considers the developmental needs of young students and how well-chosen fictional literature can enable children to understand and remember scientific concepts. It presents criteria for judging such books and suggests appropriate activities for their use. It also suggests ways to work with school library media centers and specialists in selecting materials. A sample unit presents a classic children's book as basis for a science unit in the classroom. An annotated bibliography lists children's literature relevant to the study of science, technology, and society.

The remainder of the book provides specific activities for teachers to use in the classroom, suggesting 33 children's books that are easily adapted to the elementary curriculum. Parts II, III, and IV cover life science, earth and space science, and physical science, respectively. An answer key for puzzles presented in the chapters is found in the Appendix.

Part I
USING CHILDREN'S LITERATURE AS A
SPRINGBOARD TO SCIENCE

1

INTEGRATING SCIENCE
AND READING

Fictional literature can be used as the foundation of science instruction. Because literature has a story line, children may find it easier to follow the ideas that are part of a plot than to comprehend facts as presented in a textbook. Science is very abstract for youngsters and must be seen as part of their own personal world if it is to be understood and remembered. The story does this by putting facts and concepts into a form that encourages children to build a hypothesis, predict events, and test to determine whether their ideas are correct. In this way, the lesson becomes relevant and conceptually in tune with the child's abilities.

This method is best conveyed through an integrated lesson that involves reading, writing, language arts, and science, as well as math, social sciences, creative arts, and physical activities. It is not necessary to limit stories to interpretation along one avenue. Anderson and other members of the Commission on Reading indicate that "the most logical place for instruction in most reading and thinking strategies is in social sciences and science rather than in separate lessons about reading. The reason is that the strategies are useful mainly when the student is grappling with important but unfamiliar content" (Anderson, et al., 1984). The strategies employed in "learning to read" and "learning science" are very similar, e.g., observing, comparing, measuring, using time/space relationships, interpreting, communicating, predicting outcomes, making judgments, and evaluation (Alexander, 1985).

For the child in the primary school, the use of children's literature in the classroom can serve as a catalyst to link these skills. By breaking down the artificial barriers of subjects as individual units locked into specific time frames, the strategies and processes that are basic to science and reading can be employed to facilitate learning in both areas.

Children's fictional literature is very appealing and fascinating for primary children. It may be a more efficient means of teaching because students' interest is sustained and the story structure helps them to comprehend and draw relationships. For example, trees are a common sight for most children. A nonfiction book or chapter dealing with trees and their uses can become totally objective, abstract, and stripped of relevance to the child's world. It might be more appropriate to use a fiction work such as Janice Udry's *A Tree Is Nice* or Shel Silverstein's *The Giving Tree*, which explains the concept of "treeness" in terms of the effect on the child's reality.

The major purpose for studying science should be to comprehend the conceptual basis of the everyday things that constitute our world. The strategies and process skills needed to understand and interpret the scientific world are more significant than specific facts (Blosser, 1986).

The goal of science instruction is to learn to solve problems. During this process, the emphasis must be on opportunities to make first-hand observations and inferences that can be communicated in a variety of ways. Children need to be allowed to make mistakes, and should be given opportunities for self-correction as they learn to comprehend. They should not be trained to merely repeat specific information, but to restate ideas from their own manipulation of objects and words, in terms that make sense to their own world.

2

SCIENCE IN THE CLASSROOM

Typically, science is taught using traditional textbooks and worksheets. Subject matter is broken into isolated bits bearing little meaning and relevance to the child's life (McCutcheon and Burton, 1981). Concept and practical application of ideas are often found omitted or touched so briefly that children develop misconceptions about science (Eaton, Anderson, and Smith, 1983). Vocabulary, a major element of comprehension, is typically taught for its own sake. Students often view texts as dull, irrelevant, and unreadable (Dole and Johnson, 1981). Teachers may regard books as so many pages to cover, while their pupils tally how many tasks they must complete in each lesson. The result is often boredom for students. Watching and performing experiments will not satisfy the needs of students unless they have learned the language and thinking intrinsic to science (Guerra and Payne, 1981). Hands-on projects such as SCIS (Science Curriculum Improvement Study, 1974) will still produce lack of comprehension if misconceptions are not addressed and new concepts explained and made relevant (Eaton, Anderson, and Smith, 1983).

We are living in an age of science and technology, yet the building blocks of knowledge that lead to an understanding of these areas receive little emphasis until students are well into their academic careers. While we do not expect children to fully understand the intricacies of a technological society, we must provide them with an early understanding and appreciation of science. Science must be taught as soon as youngsters enter school. Preschool is not too soon, but especially during the first three or four years of school the child should be exposed to scientific methods.

Just when our need for scientific and technological literacy is greatest, students are turning away from these fields. This concern has been raised in all areas of society, not just academics. Industrial leaders stress the need, not only for outstanding scientists and engineers, but for citizens who will not be bewildered by scientific change (Rothman, 1987). Government officials emphasize the importance of the United States being a technological leader capable of implementing that technology to further educate students (Sununu, 1986).

Other studies uphold these conclusions, finding that by the end of middle school, most students view science as uninteresting (Stake and Easley, 1979). It is considered too abstract and discipline-oriented; this alienates many pupils.

Researchers and leaders in the field of science education have called elementary science a "vanishing species" (Rowe, 1980). This is based on data that indicates the following:

1. Science is disappearing from the classroom, as far as time allotted for daily instruction.

2. Performance in science by nine- and thirteen-year-olds on successive National Assessments of Education Progress (NAEP) has worsened, largely because physical science knowledge has declined dramatically.

3. A substantial percentage of elementary teachers say that science and social studies are not very important for elementary students and create problems for teachers. (Facilities and trained personnel seemed to be the major items lacking.)

4. Very little money is being spent on elementary science equipment or materials.

5. Science is increasingly complex, too difficult for students to understand.

6. Young elementary students are interested in science, teachers admit, but over time they lose interest in school science.

Many questions need to be addressed concerning the status of science in American education. Why is science taught in this manner? Why do educators often see little value in teaching science? Why do students who are so curious, by nature, lose interest in science? Is science too difficult and discipline-oriented? Will increased spending on science solve the problem? When should we begin emphasizing science? Who should be taught science and what are the major goals of that instruction? How should it be taught?

Of all these questions, the last one may point to the key issue. Teaching elementary school science is not the same as teaching secondary level students, yet often the approach is basically the same. Only the difficulty of the material or the amount of work covered is significantly different.

It is important to be aware of the developmental needs of children in the early elementary grades when formulating instructional curricula. Piaget tells us that before the age of eight, children are in a preoperational stage. This has serious implications in establishing instructional curricula for elementary science (Smith, 1981). For example:

1. Children have not developed the ability to think logically or abstractly; reasoning is unsystematic and does not lead to generalizations.

2. Children can focus only on the beginning or end state of a transformation, not the transformation itself.

3. Children are not able to recognize the invariance of a number of objects when the spatial relationship of those objects is transformed.

4. Children are egocentric and view the world from their own perspective.

Others may have progressed to the concrete operational stage whereby they are able to think more consistently about the world beyond their own. Both groups view the phenomena very concretely, and they are not able to abstract information and ideas, or use formal logic to understand scientific concepts. If we try to teach children using only the realistic explanation of an adult, they are often left confused, as they cannot understand the adult's abstract reasoning process. Therefore, we need to teach in terms of children's existing knowledge and abilities, not only to foster their conceptual understanding, but to provide them with security in the immediate human environment.

No clear line separating objects and living things has yet developed for many of these youngsters, so that their thinking is often animistic—i.e., the child accepts the idea that animals can think and feel as humans do. Another element of their thinking is artificialism—everything is fashioned by humans or some other living being. Anything that cannot be explained in these terms is magic. Stories that conform to the child's own thought processes have much more meaning to them (Bettleheim, 1976). This includes the child's acceptance of fantasy. Fantasy is a situation that is contrary to reality as we know it today. It gives an extra dimension to life, for it helps push back the usual horizons of everyday living and encourages the child's creative powers. Fantasy stories typically present a universal truth such as love, hate, wisdom, and even scientific concepts. A key to children understanding reality is for them to look at their own world of fantasy and start questioning it. With the assistance of an adult, they can distinguish fantasy—the unreal—from fact, which is real.

Children will be ready to engage in rational investigations as more complicated reasoning processes develop. Scientific activity is particularly useful to enhance logical thinking and facilitate cognitive development (Piaget, 1970). It is an active method of teaching that utilizes direct instruction in reasoning. This cannot occur if we require objective thinking or abstract understanding that is beyond the child's conceptual level, any more than we can expect her or him to learn passively by observing experiments performed by the teacher. This is akin to the child's watching someone play a musical instrument and thus learning to perform the task. Science is not the stockpiling of isolated experimental results and vocabulary words, but a means of producing intellectual explorers who are not only able to reason competently at an operational level and beyond, but display a willingness to become problem solvers (Rowe, 1980).

Literature, Language, and Science

Why use children's books to teach science? Many elementary teachers feel that science itself is important, whereas teaching science in the elementary school is not. On the other hand, both reading and the instruction of reading are given prime importance. Children's literature is often a major strength and interest of teachers; they feel comfortable dealing with children's books and are used to reading them to groups. Good literature books captivate the child's interest and information is rapidly absorbed from them. Selecting a fiction book with a scientific theme, a teacher can develop a science lesson that provides both scientific information and reinforcement. This is done by reading the book to the class and using one or more hands-on activities as follow-up. Science, reading, and the language arts reinforce each other and teach the same strategies of reasoning and relationships. This integrated approach is extremely advantageous for teachers who utilize a lengthy period for reading instruction. Time is not taken away from reading class but expands the use of all literary activities in conjunction with science experiences. Any other areas of the curriculum can be integrated into the unit as desired.

Children's literature can be used in the classroom to present facts and concepts in a form that is motivating and understandable to the child (Dole and Johnson, 1981; Guerra and Payne, 1981). Well-chosen, fictional literature reinforces the idea that science is a part of the lives of ordinary people. The concepts come from a story about characters and places, which enables children to understand and remember scientific concepts more easily than a textbook approach can (Butzow and Butzow, 1988a; Butzow and Butzow, 1988b; Smardo, 1982). The story line of a book such as *Mike Mulligan and His Steam Shovel* by Virginia Lee Burton is in tune with the thought processes of the elementary student. Children can understand the concept of work and the use of machines as they follow the adventures of this book. Simple machines, force, motion, and energy can also become part of the lesson.

It is also possible to use the children's literature selection in conjunction with a school curriculum or required science book, as long as the concepts involved are compatible, and the fiction story book is not treated as a supplementary text. For example, *The Very Busy Spider* by Eric Carle can form the basis of a life science activity on spiders; *Shadows* by Blaise Cendrars teaches about the light and shadows of the earth; and chemical and physical change underlie the humor of *Strega Nona's Magic Lessons* by Tomie dePaola.

Judging Books

In choosing selections for an integrated science/reading/language arts unit, it is necessary to develop criteria by which to judge books. The following questionnaire can provide an outline for this process.

Content

Is the coverage of the book appropriate for the purpose?

Is the material within the comprehension and interest range of the age for which it was intended?

Is there an appropriate amount of detail?

Is there a balance of factual and conceptual material?

Does the book encourage curiosity and further inquiry?

Is the book connected to the curriculum content or scope of material presented in the elementary school?

Accuracy and Authenticity

Does the author's background qualify him or her to write books that include areas of science?

Are the facts and concepts presented accurately and realistically?

Are there inconsistencies in the information presented that would make the use of the book unsuitable?

Are fact and fantasy distinguished?

Is the science content of the book up-to-date?

Theme

Does the story have a theme?

Is it worth imparting?

Is the theme too obvious or overpowering?

Setting

Is the setting clearly indicated?

How is the setting relevant to the plot?

Is there a time frame delineated?

Does the time frame follow a clear temporal sequence?

Characterization

How does the author reveal the characters?

Are they convincing?

Do we see their strengths and weaknesses?

Do they act consistently with their ages?

Is there development within these characters?

Is anthropomorphism used? Is it appropriate?

Do animals retain their own characteristics?

Are the characters portrayed without racial or cultural stereotype or bias?

Plot

Does the book tell a good story? Will children enjoy it and become involved?

Is the plot fresh and plausible? Is it well constructed?

Is there a logical series of happenings? Are you prepared for the events of the book?

Is there a basis of cause and effect?

Is there an identifiable conflict, problem, or other reason to justify the actions of the characters?

Do events build to an identifiable climax?

Is there a satisfying resolution of events?

Does the story line affect the action, theme, and characters?

Style

Is there a consistent, discernible writing style appropriate to the subject?

Is the dialogue natural and balanced with narration?

Does the author create a mood? How?

Is the point of view appropriate for the book's purpose?

Is the language derogatory to any group?

Illustrations

Are the pictures an integral part of the book?

Is the action of the book reflected in the pictures?

Are the illustrations authentic, accurate, and consistent with the text?

Do they reinforce the facts and concepts expressed in the writing?

Do the pictures create and contribute to the mood of the book?

Whole Language

To integrate the teaching of reading and the teaching of science, it is advantageous to be aware of the "whole language" approach to reading and learning. With this approach, children are introduced to reading using large, purposeful units of meaning such as a literature selection. The selection is discussed, response to it is made, and activities related to it may all be carried out before the selection is broken into paragraphs, sentences, words, and letters. All reading must be in context and have meaning for the student. Individual letters and sounds are not studied in isolation and then combined into words and sentences to produce a total selection.

By "whole language" we mean that children should simultaneously learn to read for information, ideas, insights, and entertainment. In this way, students learn that print is supposed to "make sense" and can be learned naturally through experiences with writing, listening, and speaking. Strategies such as context, sentence structure, and word knowledge help them to recognize language elements. No longer are skills separated into isolated hierarchies, nor are subject areas compartmentalized. Knowledge and learning reach across the lines that divide disciplines to create a total learning experience. Just as children have learned to speak from interacting with the language they hear around them, so too do they learn to read by being placed in a literate, natural environment.

The whole language approach is based on the use of children's literature. For beginning readers, this also includes the use of books produced in large-sized versions called "big books," as well as "predictable books," which contain repeating lines or sentences that provide sufficient clues to anticipate the next words. Children are encouraged to take risks and use the context to construct the meaning of what they read. Skipping words and guessing are not frowned upon, as it encourages students to self-monitor their reading to see if it makes sense. More often than not, this results in children self-correcting their own reading.

Just as children are exposed to reading by the teacher and given time to read on their own, so too are they encouraged to begin writing, starting in kindergarten. Children keep personal dictionaries of their own words and are allowed to spell words as best they can, rather than breaking their train of thought to ask or look up a proper spelling. Self-editing of papers will take place only when children actually need to use formal grammar and spelling.

This approach is more personal and child-centered. Reading does not have to exist as a separate class, nor need there be emphasis on a controlled vocabulary, specific skills mastery, spelling and penmanship lessons, phonic analysis, or worksheets and management programs. These elements, if considered necessary, would be integrated into a much broader lesson and not taught as isolated topics (Goodman, 1986).

The whole language approach can be used across the curriculum to bring any or all subjects into a core of experiences. Some commonly used whole language activities follow.

Reading Activities

Read to children every day.

Schedule sustained silent reading for children on a regular basis.

Use partner reading—children reading aloud together or to each other.

Read additional books by the author who wrote the text for the lesson.

Read narrative and expository books on same topic.

Use "big books" and predictable books to encourage student participation in reading.

Read a biography of the author of the book.

Use assisted reading—student and teacher reading together or taking turns.

Have children read each other's writings.

Arrange for older children to read to younger children in other grades.

Have a "real world" reading corner—magazines (grownup and children's), phone books, catalogs, labels, signs, TV guides, reference books, newspapers, etc.

Set up a classroom library of recreational reading books that represent all literary genres; include books written by the children, if possible.

Read and follow recipes.

Listen to a story on tape and then read along with it.

Practice a story, then tape it.

Writing Activities

Provide for sustained silent writing time, using self-selected topics or specified ones, e.g., "If I had my choice, I would like to be ...," or "My favorite character was ...."

Write stories, including language experience stories.

Keep journals.

Keep reading logs.

Write poems and descriptions.

Draw and label maps, charts, and diagrams.

Write letters to each other, to authors, to characters in books, etc.

Sequence events of a story using words or pictures.

Employ cloze procedures to build vocabulary and context skills.

Edit each other's writing.

Rewrite or edit you own materials, using a word processor, if possible.

Predict the ending of the story and write it out.

Rewrite the story's ending or create a sequel to the existing text.

Create multiple endings for the same story and see which one is most popular.

"Publish" a class newspaper.

Adapt stories into radio dramas, plays, TV programs.

Write book reviews.

Summarize the story for a book jacket or bulletin board display which you make.

Think of interview questions to ask a guest who will visit the class.

Rewrite the major action of the story from the viewpoint of another character in the book.

Keep personal dictionaries of key words from stories or words of special interest.

Make up or complete word searches, crossword puzzles, word games, acrostics, etc. that are related to the lesson.

Learn to write out directions and have someone follow them.

Keep a card file of all books read by children and the teacher on each major topic; categorize them as fiction and non-fiction.

Make a question box to hold inquiries on topic being studied; once a week, open the box and answer the questions.

Write up scientific experiments and results.

Make time lines using long sheets of shelf paper or heavy twine knotted every few inches to represent a certain number of years.

Have a letter-writing corner and a post office; use milk carton mailboxes so each child can receive mail.

Put written signs on items in room — use single words and short phrases.

Write out and attach directions for plant care, animal feeding, etc.

Post explanations or rules for fire drills, going to the library, special class changes, etc.

Set up bulletin boards, attendance sheets, job charts, and sign-up rosters which students can maintain.

Provide a message board for communication to the teacher and to other students.

Have a grocery or regular store, including sales slips, shopping lists, and empty cans and boxes with the labels attached.

Make a gallery of children's and teachers' biographies — attach recent or baby photos.

Set up a weather station including devices to measure temperature, wind speed, and wind direction; study daily weather maps from the newspaper; have materials on hand to measure and record local sky, wind, and precipitation conditions.

Use calendars to keep track of classroom events, or have annotated ones indicating famous events, birthdays, honorary weeks, etc.

Discussion Topics

Children can retell a story as a comprehension check.

Use direct instruction and modeling to gain insight into text components (such as plot, setting, character, theme) or skills such as inference, cause and effect, prediction, sequence, comparison, and drawing conclusions.

Hold panel discussions and debates.

Conduct interviews and discussions with outside speakers, each other, or "characters from the book."

Practice and give oral book reviews (NOT book reports).

Play "Who Said That?" to identify important lines from book or "This Is Your Life" to review the accomplishments of the characters.

Think of new titles for a book and discuss if they are meaningful.

What other facts do you want to know about the topic? How can you find them? Check out your ideas.

Learn about the historical and geographical setting of the story if it is integral to the concepts of the story.

What was the author's purpose for writing this book?

Art

Make cartoons of the action in the story and sequence them.

Draw pictures depicting characters or events in the story.

Design book jackets.

Make advertisements or bulletin boards about the book or its scientific concepts.

Write a commercial to encourage people to buy or read "your" book.

Build dioramas or paint murals suggested by the setting of the book.

Design a coat of arms for a major character using symbols to show the accomplishments of his or her life.

Label exhibits and collections of objects pertaining to the book.

Sketch or make costumes similar to those of the characters (use dolls or people as your model).

Show photos or slides to provide background knowledge of the book.

Make "movie rolls" from shelf paper and paper toweling tubes.

Construct puppets from paper bags, felt, or papier mâché.

Assemble a collage of pictures showing concepts and/or events in the story.

Invent a competitive board game about the story; include questions on vocabulary, events, characters, sequences, etc.

Bring in current magazine and newspaper articles that have relevance to story.

Initiate a fan club for your favorite author or character; include membership cards, buttons, newsletters, etc. (Marc Brown's Arthur has his own fan club.)

Drama and Media

Present choral readings; include ones for large groups, sections of the class, or soloists.

Tape dramatizations in the style of the old radio shows.

Produce videotapings in which the story is acted out.

Pantomime events or concepts of the story.

Improvise or role play a section of the story, an alternate ending, scientific happening, etc.

Compare the book to a record, filmstrip, or video of the same story.

If the book is long enough, serialize it and present it over several days.

Pretend to be a movie director and cast the characters in the book for TV or a film.

Practice, then give dramatic readings.

Select appropriate music to go with the reading or dramatization.

The goals of the whole language approach and scientific method are very similar and warrant close comparison. In both cases, the child looks at the entire passage and then builds generalizations. By using storybooks, children can question, even when they are still too young to design and carry out experiments with formal logic and draw conclusions from them. For early childhood instruction in science, a more right-brain-oriented, concrete, creative method can assist children to organize their experiences and observations into meaningful learning experiences. In the following chart, traditionally used methodology that emphasizes recall of specific information is described as "fact science," in contrast to a more conceptually based approach that corresponds to the whole language philosophy.

Whole Science	Fact Science
Conceptually oriented	Recall of specific vocabulary emphasized
Emphasizes applications	Applications not emphasized
Emphasizes problem solving	Prepares student for later learning
Learner develops explanations	Explanations are provided
Activities precede understanding	Activities follow understanding
Motivation is paramount	Student motivation is not essential

It is necessary to plan before beginning an integrated reading/language arts/science lesson. First a book must be chosen that will fit curricular needs and the interests and abilities of students, and that will also fulfill the requirements of the book selection criteria. The teacher may enlist the aid of a library media specialist to help with this task, and also follow the recommendations of professional books and journals. These will be discussed at length in the section on library media.

After several careful readings of the book, it will be possible to sketch out the objectives and activities for the lesson or unit. The following outline form can serve as a guide:

Activities Planner

Title of Book_____

Author_____

Science concepts/facts in book_____

_____

_____

Vocabulary relevant to science_____

_____

_____

Possible activities/science _____

_____

_____

Possible activities/reading, language arts, writing_____

_____

_____

Possible activities/social studies, math, the arts, physical education_____

_____

_____

Additional comments_____

_____

_____

Concept Mapping

Research and experience both indicate that children comprehend better if there are cross links or relationships in the material presented to them. Recalling isolated facts and details is not the only purpose for reading, as this does not indicate whether children have truly comprehended the meaning or concepts contained in the text. Higher-level thinking skills are not tapped or developed when only factual recall is elicited. Learning should be the linking of concepts. In reading, it is necessary to understand not only how the specific concepts are interlinked, but to integrate the author's written text with the background and knowledge of the reader. In this way, reading becomes a process by which the learner actually constructs the meaning in his or her mind. In using literature in the classroom, it is necessary to understand that the concepts that are contained in the written materials, not just the facts and details, must be the focus of instruction. Children must be helped to recognize these concepts or ideas that the author is developing and relate them to each other, and to their own background.

This can be enhanced by a procedure known as "concept mapping," which helps learners to recognize and link concepts or ideas. "Concept maps work to make clear to both students and teachers the small number of key ideas they must focus on for any specific learning task. A map can also provide a kind of visual road map showing some of the pathways we may take to connect meanings of concepts in propositions. After a learning task has been completed, concept maps provide a schematic summary of what has been learned" (Novak and Gowan, 1984).

Concept maps are simple visual devices that allow the person to relate the major ideas in a text, a fiction book, the mind, or any other source. To make a concept map:

1. Select each major concept or idea and draw an oval around it.

2. Work down from key ideas to secondary ones, then to specific facts or examples. Each time draw an oval around the concept.

3. Join all closely related concepts with lines and write connecting verbs on the lines to explain the relationships (see figure 2.1).

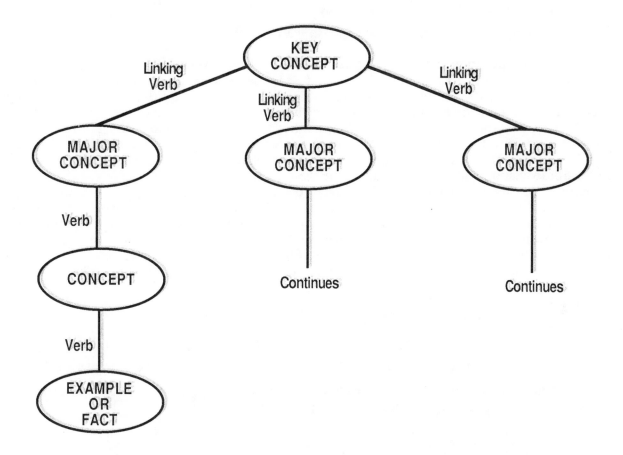

Fig. 2.1. Generic Concept Map.

There are several reasons for developing the use of concept mapping in the classroom:

1. To introduce a story or build background
2. To increase comprehension
3. To expand vocabulary
4. To review information
5. To evaluate learning progress
6. To serve as a basis for writing activities

7. To show that ideas are interconnected or radiate from a key concept, rather than ordered linearly such as in an outline

8. To help promote cooperative or group learning

It is fairly easy to determine if children are able to perform the task of concept mapping. After reading a short selection with them, the teacher can initiate a discussion about the main *ideas* of the story or the author's *purpose* for writing the piece. If the children can remember only factual information, the teacher can stimulate the conversation with questions such as Why? How? What were the results? Were there any connections between events?, etc. The next step is to work together and brainstorm one or more concept maps based on the selection. Children should see the connections and relationships, and understand that these are not facts, but ideas. Factual information will be presented only at the example stage of the map.

Once the children have seen the large picture and understand the purposes behind concept mapping, a step-by-step process can be used to teach them to recognize concepts. This can be done with youngsters from the earliest primary grades through high school. The first time children are involved in concept mapping, they can be led through the process by the teacher, who records their responses on the chalkboard. The teacher should stress the hierarchy of concepts, linking concepts, using verbs, and finding relationships if the children do not readily see them.

1. Have children visualize a specific word, write the word on the board, and draw or describe the word, e.g., flower.

2. Visualize an "event" word and write it; draw or describe it, e.g., blooming.

3. Explain that a concept is a word that means a kind of object or event "picture."

4. Emphasize that concepts can be linked by verbs or action words, and write simple sentences linking two concepts, e.g., the flower is blooming.

5. Select concept words from sentences.

6. From a list of words, differentiate "object concepts" (rose, daffodil) and "event concepts" (summer, Easter).

7. To construct a map, take a word and show the related concepts. This is somewhat like word association. Put these in a hierarchy from key concept to secondary concept to specific example (see figure 2.2).

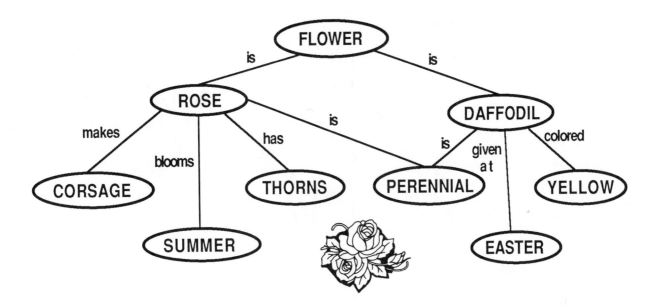

Fig. 2.2. Example concept map.

8.   See if there are any cross links or relationships. For example, both flowers are perennials.

9.   Assign a word to each child and let them try to concept map the word. Discuss various attempts.

10. Read another short selection and find the concepts. Put them in a hierarchy from primary to secondary importance. Some concepts may radiate like the spokes of a wheel.

11. Continue doing maps based on more involved materials. These can be done in large groups, small groups, or individually.

The teacher, in determining objectives for using the story, must decide which concepts will be stressed. These will be the major concepts that students should include on their concept map. Teachers can utilize a score sheet of points to check to see if students have included the key concept, general and secondary concepts, linking words, crosslinks or relations, a hierarchy or pattern, and examples. Using concept mapping in this way as an evaluation tool is somewhat subjective, since no two concept maps will be the same.

Concept mapping can be used at any stage in the instruction of reading. It can serve a variety of purposes, from building an understanding of one specific word, to the comprehension of an entire selection. The basic reason for using concept mapping remains constant, and that is to help the student use conceptual analysis and recognize and use relationships.

Figures 2.3 and 2.4 illustrate ways of mapping the concepts for *Who Sank the Boat* by Pamela Allen and *Chipmunk Song* by Joanna Ryder. These books are the subjects of chapters 12 and 28, respectively.

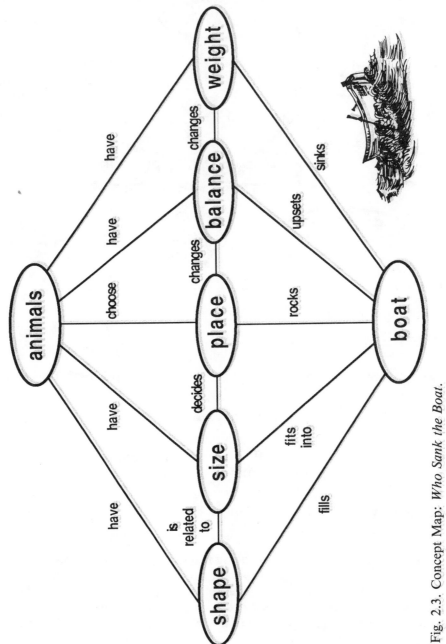

Fig. 2.3. Concept Map: *Who Sank the Boat.*

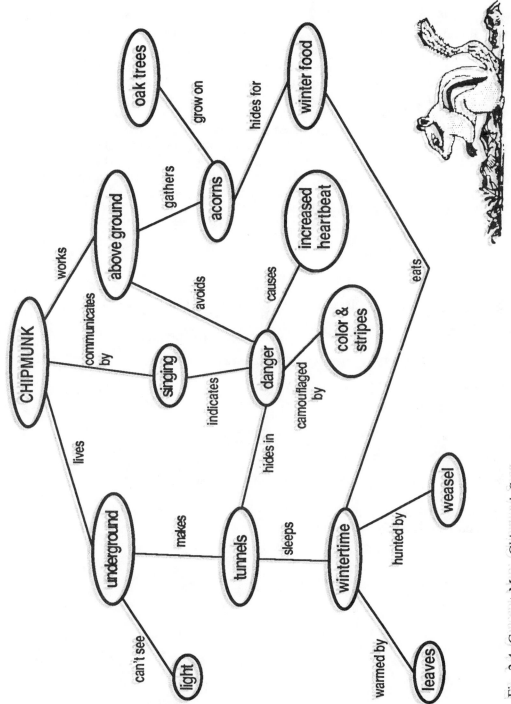

Fig. 2.4. Concept Map: *Chipmunk Song.*

Mike Mulligan and His Steam Shovel: A Sample Unit

Mike Mulligan and His Steam Shovel by Virginia Lee Burton is a classic example of children's literature. Mike, the enthusiastic steam shovel operator, symbolizes integrity, determination, and hard work. Mary Ann, his well-loved steam shovel, helps carry out any job Mike believes they can accomplish. Undaunted by the threat of more advanced machines, Mike and Mary Ann meet the challenge of digging the cellar for the Popperville town hall in a single day.

Mike and Mary Ann exemplify outstanding personal attributes and virtues, but there is much more for us to learn from these characters. First, the book is an outstanding source of scientific concepts and information, and can be used as the basis of an instructional unit on machines and energy. Second, the book is an excellent model for language arts activities and process writing classes, which can be integrated with the science instruction. Third, the underlying theme of the book, obsolescence, can be examined in terms children can easily understand. What happens when a machine becomes outdated or is replaced by a technologically advanced piece of equipment? How does technology affect the way we live? What is the effect of change in our society?

Mike Mulligan and Science

In using *Mike Mulligan and His Steam Shovel* as the basis of a science unit, it is first necessary to identify major scientific concepts contained in the book:

Machines themselves work or make work easier for people.

Machines need energy to produce movement.

Various fuel sources produce energy.

Machines can become obsolete.

It is possible for one machine to do various tasks.

Simple machines are powered by people.

Simple machines combine to become complex machines.

A pictorial representation of these concepts and their relationship to each other is shown on a concept map in figure 2.5.

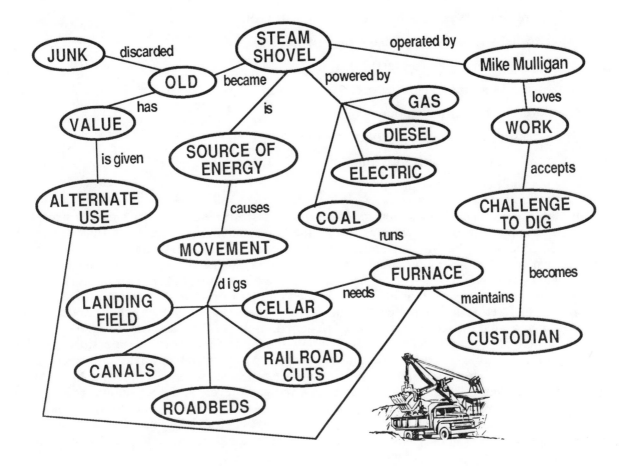

Fig. 2.5. Concept Map: *Mike Mulligan and His Steam Shovel.*

This list of concepts and the map can serve as a guide for the teacher throughout the unit. The first activity might be an investigation of the use of simple machines to help stimulate interest as well as to show the application of machines to everyday life.

Each child is given an index card bearing an item, along with an instruction. For example:

(a) a nail pounded into a piece of wood at an angle/remove nail and pound in straight

(b) a piece of wood with a screw in it/remove screw

(c) a rough stick of wood/make it smooth

(d) an egg white/whip it until stiff

(e) a carrot/peel it

 (f) a ball of yarn/crochet a chain

 (g) a dressmaker's pattern pinned on cloth/cut it out

 (h) two flat sticks/glue into shape of a sword

 (i) a ball of yarn/make a scarf

 (j) a cork in a bottle/remove cork

 (k) wire/cut a specified amount

 (l) a plastic or metal can/pry open the top

 (m) a piece of cheese/slice very thinly

 (n) a small board/saw it in half

In order to perform the task mentioned on the card, it is necessary to use an implement. On a large table, make a display of various household tools, including extra ones that will not be needed. Include pliers, hammers, screwdrivers, wrenches, wire cutters, small crow bar, scissors, saw, garden trowel, wire whip, carrot peeler, C clamp, crochet hook, knitting needles, bottle opener, corkscrew, wood plane, wire cheese slicer, and pizza cutter. Perhaps a mystery could be added if one is available, such as an old-fashioned curling iron or a shoe button hook.

Let the children select an implement and perform the task. Discuss why they chose that particular item and what movement it produced to help do the job. Would another tool have worked as well, or better? From this demonstration of how the implements work, it is possible to deduce the six simple machines—wedge, lever, pulley, inclined plane, wheel and axle, and screw. Other items not used can also be observed and a tool that combines several simple machines can be analyzed; for example, a hand can opener uses a wedge, a lever, and a wheel and axle.

The story of *Mike Mulligan and His Steam Shovel* can be read to the group or shown on slides or video. You may wish to do this two or three times before beginning a general discussion of what the story was about, and what the children learned about machines. The following science-oriented activities can be used:

1. On a bulletin board display, identify and label simple machines that are part of a steam shovel.

2. Discuss machines with family members and share the information with the class, e.g.: How have machines changed in your parents' or grandparents' lifetime? Are there old machines around the house or garage? Do machines ever cause problems?

3. Design and make a machine using plastic or wooden construction toys and be able to explain the purpose of the machine.

4. Investigate the school's energy supply. Why is this fuel source used? What are the energy costs for the year? Charts and graphs can be compiled from this information. Figure 2.6 is a chart showing energy costs for a school. It can be adapted to any school.

ANNUAL ENERGY COST

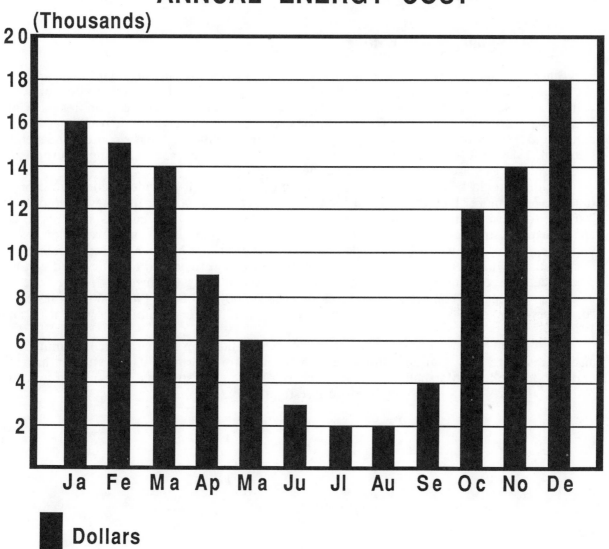

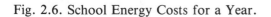 **Dollars**

Fig. 2.6. School Energy Costs for a Year.

5. Read other fiction books about machines, and have catalogs about tools, machines, autos, etc. available during free time or recess. Can you identify the simple machines?

6. Use pulleys or boards to move heavy objects.

Mike Mulligan and Writing

Since reading and writing strategies are utilized in both science and language arts, they should not be taught as separate subjects (Anderson, et al., 1985). The integration of science with other disciplines enables students to become critical thinkers and decisionmakers (Gates, Krockover, and Wiedermann, 1987) and emphasizes the relation between the teaching of subject matter and instruction in process skills. Problem-solving activities cannot be content-independent (Hodson, 1988). All reading and writing should be done as a means to achieving a purpose, and not as isolated exercises that are an end in themselves.

Writing should be a major element in learning science for it provides a continuous opportunity to learn more about the topic during the actual act of composing. In this way, students are "writing to learn" instead of the traditional "learning to write." This enables students to concretely express strategies such as observation, description, comparison, and evaluation. Representing experiences in words helps students to form relationships between concepts and/or ideas (Marshall, 1987; Kucer, 1985). As students continue writing, they read to review and edit each piece. Ideas are formulated, tested, and reflected upon to bring full meaning to the text. This improves concept and comprehension development (Tierney and Leys, 1986). Writing becomes a "discovery function"—i.e., you do not know what something means until you write it (Brandt, 1986).

Writing can be a superior means of examining what students have learned from a unit. Short-answer tests are very limiting, and give little chance to determine if the student has truly understood the text (Marshall, 1987). A daily journal can aid students in reviewing and summarizing the activities of each day's lesson (see figure 2.7).

today we wacthed a film called Mike mulgens steam shovel. We learned that machines can do more worke than poeple can do in one day. I like the story mike mulgens steam shovel it's one of my faverites.

Fig. 2.7. An Entry from Jayme's Journal.

A second major writing activity is to have the children compose an alternative ending for the book. In the original story, Mary Ann, the steam shovel, remains in the cellar to become the furnace for the town hall while Mike assumes the role of janitor. To write an ending that would involve a workable solution to the problem of extricating the steam shovel from the cellar it had dug or to create another possible ending, students must show an understanding of concepts about machinery and work and devise ways to utilize simple or complex machines to solve the problem. The conclusion should be realistic and in keeping with the rest of the book. This eliminates the use of futuristic machines, robots, etc., which might have little connection with the concepts covered during the unit (see figure 2.8).

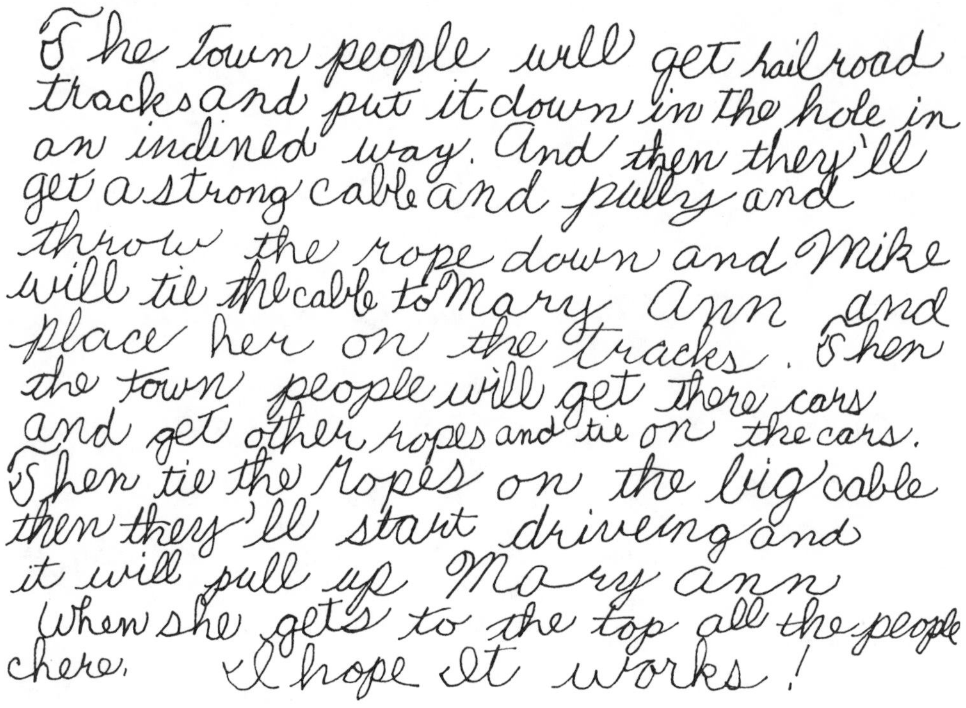

The town people will get railroad tracks and put it down in the hole in an inclined way. And then they'll get a strong cable and pulley and throw the rope down and Mike will tie the cable to Mary Ann and place her on the tracks. Then the town people will get there cars and get other ropes and tie on the cars. Then tie the ropes on the big cable then they'll start driving and it will pull up Mary Ann When she gets to the top all the people there. I hope It works!

Fig. 2.8. Edward's Alternative Ending.

Students should be allowed to brainstorm ideas before they begin writing. In keeping with the process writing approach (Graves, 1983) teachers should conference with students during the writing time, and allow students to read and conference each other's work. Only after the piece has been rewritten and is ready to be "published" should attention be given to the mechanics of grammar and spelling for the final copy.

Mike Mulligan and Change

A third area of study using this book is suggested by the sentence "Mike took such good care of Mary Ann she never grew old." This introduces the concepts of aging and change. Society is not constant, for every human activity alters the environment and produces change. The only constant that does exist, therefore, is the fact that change will occur. We cannot always control whether change should take place. Instead we must examine whether it is an indication of progress and growth, and decide if these new alternatives are beneficial and acceptable. Students must cope with a world of change based on increasing knowledge and technological advances. Society values technology because it increases efficiency and lessens the effort we must make. These are assumed to be desirable traits, for our economy is based on the idea that time is money.

Mike had to face the fact that even though Mary Ann was still beautiful and could do the necessary work, more efficient machines were being employed. Only when Mike claimed to be able to dig a cellar in one day was credibility given to an "old" machine, because, again, time is money. Despite their success, modern alternatives would still eliminate Mary Ann's usefulness as a steam shovel. Fortunately, the steam boiler that once provided mechanical energy (movement) to the shovel could be converted to produce heat energy in a furnace.

Several activities can help youngsters understand the role of change in their lives:

1. Study old photos of the community to see changes in transportation, housing, clothing, geographic features, etc.

2. Interview older persons to learn how lifestyles have changed, e.g., schooling, occupations, recreation, church, use of appliances, etc.

3. Bring in examples of less technologically advanced objects—egg beater, hand can opener, manual adding machine, crystal radio set, etc. What are the similarities and differences with more modern items?

4. Assume your town has an old, run-down, but historic area. Developers wish to tear it down for a shopping mall. What are the options available? For example, allow the plan to be implemented, revitalize the area for business and shopping, restore only the historical buildings, and build new ones in between. This could be presented through debates, speeches, sketches, etc.

5. What happens to material objects that are no longer needed, e.g., lawn sales, recycling, disposal. This might raise the issues of sanitary landfill, pollution, litter, toxic wastes.

6. Decide what life might be like at a certain time in the future. Write descriptions of this society and design cities or machines that will need to exist then.

7. Make a chart of items that have become obsolete in the last 50 years (e.g., a scrub board, crank telephones, the ice box, etc.) and items which you think will become obsolete in the next 50 years (e.g., manual typewriters, glass bottles, coin and paper money, libraries of books, etc.). A third column might inolve things that will become everyday necessities during this time (e.g., nonfossil fuel transportation devices, picture telephones, pocket-sized computers, etc.).

8. Compare the way inanimate objects become old with the way people age. Numerous works of children's literature are available at all levels on the topics of growing old and dying. For example, three different lifestyles for older people are represented in the picture books *I Know An Old Lady* by Charlotte Zolotow, *Nana Upstairs and Nana Downstairs* by Tomie dePaola, and *My Grandma's in a Nursing Home* by Judy Delton and Dorothy Tucker.

Science, Technology, and Society (STS)

The integration of various subject matter disciplines and process skills as exemplified above is the goal of a contemporary movement called Science, Technology, and Society (STS). The purpose of STS is to empower learners to make judgments about the role of science and technology in the daily life of their society. This integrated approach assists in developing problem-solving skills by analyzing situations that affect choices and human values. The complexity of today's societal issues confront children long before they are capable of abstract thought. Using stories that deal with topics such as change and obsolescence, as well as water resources, air quality, nuclear war, human health, and plant and animal extinction, enables teachers to introduce these ideas and incorporate science and technology in a way that has meaning to the child. By integrating ideas, writing, language arts, and social studies, instruction time in each area is enhanced. Learning is facilitated since skills and strategies have practical application to everyday life.

The following areas of concern have been identified as important in the study of Science, Technology, and Society (Bybee, 1987). These topics should be introduced beginning in the lower elementary grades and continue throughout the child's school years as a means of preparing them to understand and/or help alleviate the problems of the technological world in which they will live.

Population growth

World hunger and food resources (agriculture)

Human health and disease (diet, stress, noise, pollution effects, epidemics)

Water resources

Air quality and atmosphere

Land use (erosion)

Extinction of plants and animals (wildlife protection)

Mineral resources (mining, technology, recycling)

Energy shortage

Hazardous substances (chemicals, dumps, lead paints)

War technology

Nuclear reactors and power

Technological advances (in transportation, communication, manufacturing, automation, etc.)

Library Media

Working with the school library media specialist makes the job of the classroom teacher much easier. The specialist is trained in many areas: gathering and disseminating materials, teaching small and large groups as well as individuals, and utilizing and producing audiovisual materials.

Traditionally science has been considered as a topic for nonfiction writing. As a result, the scientific facts and concepts in a fiction work are often passed over because people are not specifically looking for them or because their accuracy is doubted. A connection between fiction books and scientific concepts must be established as topics and skills are linked into units. The specialist can assist in doing this and is an excellent source for locating fiction books with scientific themes, either in the school's library media center or in a community or university center. Books not available in the school library can often be obtained through interlibrary loan.

When first working with the specialist, it would be best for the teacher to share several fiction books being considered as the basis for integrated science units. This will give the teacher a change to discuss the type of books that would be suitable for those units. If possible, the specialist should be given a broad range of topics, or a list of prospective titles, so he or she can begin compiling a selection of available works. Because the specialist has the expertise to select worthwhile books and eliminate those of questionable value, the teacher will be able to devote this time to planning activities.

Once topics are selected, book clusters on similar topics may emerge. For example, *Sadie and the Snowman* by Allan Morgan, *The Snowy Day* by Ezra Jack Keats, *The Big Snow* by Berta Hader and Elmer Hader, and *Katy and the Big Snow* by Virginia Lee Burton would each be suitable as the basis of a lesson. Topics that are interrelated are useful. A reference to spiders in *Two Bad Ants* by Chris Van Allsburg might be followed by *The Very Busy Spider* by Eric Carle. Author clusters are a third possibility. Robert McCloskey writes of life along the Maine coast; Leo Lionni and Eric Carle explore scientific truths and human values through the fantasy animals they have created; Virginia Lee Burton is expert on picturing the plight of objects in a growing, often polluted world; and Dr. Seuss has us pondering the fate of humanity and the environment.

As more information is needed to augment the original book, nonfiction books can be gathered together for sustained silent reading time, at-home reading, or classroom reference. These sources are imperative if children wish to do further research on a topic or answer specific questions that have evolved from classroom discussions or activities. The specialist can address research skills in a teaching lesson, thereby emphasizing or reinforcing materials covered in the classroom and facilitating students' searches for additional information. The specialist can engage in cooperative teaching to assist in the transfer of learning for students, by addressing a previously covered issue from a different perspective or in a different setting. For example, concept mapping done in the classroom might be reinforced in the library media center using different materials or books to emphasize the importance of this tool.

Although the use of books is of prime importance in this integrated approach, many forms of media now exist which allow stories to be more easily seen and heard by large groups, or used for individual or small group work. Films, filmstrip/tapes, book/records, book/tapes, and videos are available for many classic works of children's literature. Specialists have access to information about these materials and have the expertise to preview and select those which they consider both useful and of high quality. The specialist who knows of teacher interest in these items may also have discretionary funds to purchase some of them. The production of audiovisual materials within the school has become much easier and efficient in recent years. The specialist is often able to assist or train others in the production of videos, slides, tapes, "big books," etc.

The specialist may possess or have access to many other materials that can enhance the unit—pictures, posters, commercial kits designed around the book in use, puppets, specimens or collections of objects such as small rocks, butterflies, etc. An aquarium, terrarium, or small animal habitat that may be a permanent part of the center can become an excellent mini field trip. Displays and learning centers can be set up to correspond with a particular integrated unit.

The search for printed text and information on specific subjects has become much more efficient with on-line computer searches. Many schools possess these facilities while others may have easy access to them. A personal computer is often an integral part of the library media center. Available software may complement your unit and help children practice thinking skills while reinforcing the lesson.

One of the most important sources of information the specialist can share is the collection of professional books and journals for librarians. While these may be readily available to teachers, space often dictates that they be in the specialist's office or other less available spot. To find books by title, author, or specific subject, refer to the Brodart Company's *Elementary School Library Collection: A Guide to Books and Other Media* or Carolyn Leina's *A to Zoo: Subject Access to Children's Picture Books*. Professional library journals such as *Booklist, Horn Book,* and *School Library Journal* publish reviews of children's books. More topically centered books are reviewed in publications like *The Reading Teacher, Language Arts, Science and Children*, and *School Science and Mathematics*.

Many magazines published for children include all areas of the curriculum. Those with wide appeal like *Cricket* would contain articles in subject areas as well as stories. Other magazines are specifically aimed at science and nature, e.g. *National Geographic World, Ranger Rick, Chickadee*, and *Owl*.

Finding books to suit specific needs becomes an ongoing process for the teacher, as there are always additional units to be developed and new, exciting books to use. In addition to all the resources of the library media center and the specialist, one should visit book fairs, join children's book clubs, and go to children's book stores. These stores often send out newsletters listing new books, author biographies, and activities at the store.

Networking is another means of locating books. At conferences, workshops, or meetings, teachers may meet others with similar interests and exchange bibliographies. Talking with teachers, browsing in the library, keeping abreast of award-winning books each year, mentioning it to friends who read to their children, and educational television programs such as *Reading Rainbow* can all be sources of new books.

There are no definitive bibliographies to help locate books for an integrated unit, and there is no teacher's manual written to indicate the steps to follow for a lesson. But there is much more to recommend the integrated approach. The creativity and enthusiasm of a teacher who follows this path can have immediate, positive results on students.

Learning does not consist of lists to be read, memorized, and given back to the teacher on a test. Learning is the acquisition of knowledge. It is a change in behavior, an education for the present and for the future. Children can learn for the moment, but they are also developing the skills and strategies they will need for the future. This process is not restricted to isolated subjects, but integrates all the areas of the curriculum and enables the student to see relationships between them.

Bibliography

References Cited

Alexander, Gretchen M., and Lisa K. Alexander. "Science and Reading: Partners in Learning." Paper presented at the National Science Teachers' Association Convention, Cincinnati, Ohio (1985).

Anderson, Richard C., Elfrieda H. Hiebert, Judith A. Scott, and Ian A. G. Wilkinson. *Becoming a Nation of Readers: The Report of the Commission on Reading.* Washington, D.C.: U.S. Department of Education, 1984.

Bettleheim, Bruno. *The Uses of Enchantment: The Meaning and Importance of Fairy Tales.* New York: Alfred A. Knopf, 1976.

Brandt, Deborah. "Social Foundations of Reading and Writing." In *Convergences*, edited by Bruce Peterson. Urbana, Ill.: National Council of Teachers of English, 1986.

Blosser, Patricia. "What Research Says: Improving Science Education." *School Science and Mathematics* 86 (November, 1986): 597-612.

Butzow, Carol M., and John W. Butzow. "Using *The Black Pearl* and Other Fictional Literature in Middle School Science." *School Science and Mathematics* 88 (March, 1988a): 236-41.

_____. "Facts from Fiction." *Science and Children* 25 (March, 1988b): 27-29.

Bybee, Roger. "Teaching about Science-Technology-Society (STS): Views of Science Educators in the United States." *School Science and Mathematics* 87 (April, 1987): 274-85.

Dole, Janice A., and Virginia R. Johnson. "Beyond the Textbook: Science Literature for Young People." *Journal of Reading* 24 (1981): 579-82.

Eaton, Janet, Charles Anderson, and Edward Smith. *Students' Misconceptions Interfere with Learning: Case Studies of Fifth Grade Students.* Lansing: Michigan State University, Institute for Research on Teaching, 1983.

Gates, Richard, Gerald Krockover, and Robert Wiedermann. "Elementary Student Teachers' Perceptions of Science in Their Classrooms: 1985-86," *School Science and Mathematics* 87 (December, 1987): 633-44.

Goodman, Kenneth. *What's Whole in Whole Language?* Portsmouth, N.H.: Heinemann Educational Books, 1986.

Graves, Donald. *Writing: Teachers and Children at Work.* Portsmouth, N.H.: Heinemann Educational Books, 1983.

Guerra, Cathy L., and DeLores B. Payne. "Using Popular Books and Magazines to Interest Students in General Science." *Journal of Reading* 24 (1981): 583-85.

Hodson, Derek. "Toward a Philosophically More Valid Science Curriculum." *Science Education* 72 (January, 1988): 19-40.

Kucer, Stephen. "The Making of Meaning: Reading and Writing as Parallel Processes." *Written Communication* 2 (July, 1985): 317-36.

Marshall, James. "The Effects of Writing on Students' Understanding of Literary Texts." *Research in the Teaching of English* 21 (February, 1987): 30-58.

McCutcheon, Gail, and Frederick Burton. *A Qualitative Study of Children's Responses to Textbook Centered Classrooms* (Research/technical 143). Columbus: Ohio State University, 1981.

Novak, Joseph, and D. Bob Gowan. *Learning How to Learn*. Cambridge, England: Cambridge University Press, 1984.

Piaget, Jean. *Science of Education and the Psychology of the Child*. New York: Orion Press, 1970.

Rothman, Robert. "Shift in Science-Education Focus Urged." *Education Week* no. 29 (1987): 7.

Rowe, Mary Budd. "Elementary Science: A Vanishing Species." *Science and Children* 14 (1980): 19-21.

Science Curriculum Improvement Study (SCIS). Berkeley, Calif.: Lawrence Hall of Science, 1974. Currently available in reprint from Delta Education, Nashua, N.H.

Smardo, Frances A. "Using Children's Literature to Clarify Science Concepts in Early Childhood Programs." *Reading Teacher* 36 (1982): 267-73.

Smith, Robert. "Early Childhood Science Education." *Young Children* 36 (1981): 3-10.

Spache, George D., and Evelyn B. Spache. *Reading in the Elementary School*. 5th ed. Boston: Allyn and Bacon, 1986.

Stake, Robert E., and Jack A. Easley. *Case Studies in Science Education* (NSF Contract No. 7621134). Washington, D.C.: U.S. Government Printing Office Stock No. 038-000-00364-0, 1979.

Sununu, John. "Will Technologies Make Learning and Teaching Easier?" *Phi Delta Kappan* 68, no. 4 (1986): 220-222.

Tierney, Robert, and Marjorie Leys. "What Is the Value of Connecting Reading and Writing?" In *Convergences*, edited by Bruce Peterson. Urbana, Ill.: National Council of Teachers of English, 1986.

Reading and Whole Language References

Goodman, Kenneth. *What's Whole in Whole Language?* Portsmouth, N.H.: Heinemann Educational Books, 1986.

Hansen, Jane, Thomas Newkirk, and Donald Graves, eds. *Breaking Ground*. Portsmouth, N.H.: Heinemann Educational Books, 1985.

Harste, Jerome, Virginia Woodward, and Carolyn Burke. *Language Stories and Literacy Lessons*. Portsmouth, N.H.: Heinemann Educational Books, 1984.

Holdaway, Don. *The Foundations of Literacy*. Portsmouth, N.H.: Heinemann Educational Books, 1979.

Huck, Charlotte, and Doris Kuhn. *Children's Literature in the Elementary School*. 4th ed. New York: Holt, Rinehart and Winston, 1987.

Newman, Judith M., ed. *Whole Language Theory in Use*. Portsmouth, N.H.: Heinemann Educational Books, 1985.

Smith, Frank. *Reading without Nonsense*. 2d ed. New York: Teachers College, Columbia University, 1985.

Science Activity Books

Abruscato, Joseph, and Jack Hassard. *The Earth People Activity Book: People, Places, Pleasures and Other Delights*. Glenview, Ill.: Scott, Foresman and Co., 1978.

_____. *The Whole Cosmos Catalog of Science Activities*. Glenview, Ill.: Scott, Foresman and Co., 1978.

Comstock, Anna B. *Handbook of Nature-Study*. Ithaca, N.Y.: Cornell University Press, 1986.

Cornell, Joseph B. *Sharing Nature with Children*. Nevada City, Calif.: Dawn Publications, 1979.

DeBruin, Jerry. *Creative, Hands-on Science Experiences*. Carthage, Ill.: Good Apple, 1986.

Gardner, Martin. *Entertaining Science Experiments with Everyday Objects*. New York: Dover Publications, 1981.

Hanauer, Ethel. *Biology Experiments for Children*. New York: Dover Publications, 1968.

Lowery, Lawrence, and Carol Verbeeck. *Explorations in Earth Science*. Belmont, Calif.: David S. Lake Publishers, 1987.

_____. *Explorations in Life Science*. Belmont, Calif.: David S. Lake Publishers, 1987.

_____. *Explorations in Physical Science*. Belmont, Calif.: David S. Lake Publishers, 1987.

Mitchel, John, ed. *The Curious Naturalist*. Englewood, Cliffs, N.J.: Prentice-Hall, 1980.

Mullin, Virginia L. *Chemistry Experiments for Children*. New York: Dover Publications, Inc., 1968.

Outdoor Biology Instructional Strategies (OBIS). Nashua, N.H.: Delta Education, 1982.

Pilger, Mary Anne. *Science Experiments Index for Young People*. Englewood, Colo.: Libraries Unlimited, 1988. (Available in print version and on computer data disk)

Reuben, Gabriel. *Electricity Experiments for Children*. New York: Dover Publications, 1968.

Vivian, Charles. *Science Experiments and Amusements for Children*. New York: Dover Publications, 1967.

Standard Bibliographies of Children's Literature

Arbuthnot, May Hill. *Children's Books Too Good to Miss*. 8th ed. Cleveland, Ohio: Press of Case Western Reserve University, 1989.

The Children's Catalog. New York: H. W. Wilson, Co.

Cranciolo, Patricia. *Picture Books for Children*. Chicago: American Library Association, 1973.

Deason, Hilary. *The AAAS Science Booklist for Children*. Washington, D.C.: American Association for the Advancement of Science, 1983.

Eakin, Mary. *Subject Index to Books for Primary Grades*. 3d ed. Chicago: American Library Association, 1967.

The Elementary School Library Collection. 15th ed. Williamsport, Pa.: Brodart, 1986.

Gillespie, John. *Elementary School Paperback Collection*. Chicago: American Library Association, 1985.

Gillespie, John, and Christine Gilbert. *Best Books for Children: Preschool through the Middle Grades*. 2d ed. New York: R. R. Bowker, 1981.

Leina, Carolyn. *A to Zoo: Subject Access to Children's Picture Books*. New York: R. R. Bowker, 1982.

Subject Guide to Books in Print. New York: R. R. Bowker, 1981.

Sutherland, Zena, ed. *Best in Children's Books, 1966-1972*. Chicago: University of Chicago Press, 1973.

_____. ed. *Best in Children's Books, 1973-1978*. Chicago: University of Chicago Press, 1980.

_____. ed. *Best in Children's Books, 1979-1984*. Chicago: University of Chicago Press, 1986.

Trelease, Jim. *The Read Aloud Handbook*. New York: Penguin Books, 1985.

Professional Journals and Children's Magazines

Booklist. American Library Association, Chicago, Ill. Published semimonthly.

Chickadee. Young Naturalist Foundation, Des Moines, Iowa. Published 10 times a year.

Cricket: the Magazine for Children. Open Court, Boulder, Colo. Published monthly.

Hornbook. Horn Book Inc., Boston, Mass. Published 6 times a year.

Language Arts. National Council of Teachers of English, Urbana, Ill. Published 7 times a year.

National Geographic World. National Geographic Society, Washington, D.C. Published monthly.

Owl, the Discovery Magazine for Children. Young Naturalist Foundation, Des Moines, Iowa. Published 10 times a year.

Ranger Rick. National Wildlife Foundation, Vienna, Va. Published monthly.

The Reading Teacher. International Reading Association, Newark, Del. Published 9 times a year.

School Library Journal. Bowker, New York, N.Y. Published 10 times a year.

School Science and Mathematics. School Science and Mathematics Association, Bowling Green, Ohio. Published 8 times a year.

Science and Children. National Science Teachers' Association, Washington, D.C. Published 8 times a year.

An Annotated Bibliography of Children's Literature Relevant to the Study of Science, Technology, and Society

Aardema, Verna. *Bringing the Rain to Kapiti Plain*. New York: Dial Books for Children, 1981. (An African legend shows the impact of drought on an agricultural society, and gives insight into the use of land during good times.)

Birch, David. *The King's Chessboard*. New York: Dial Books for Young Readers, 1988. (This tale of ancient India is a good introduction to the population explosion, as it explains the enormity of the results when each number doubles in quantity—geometric progesssion.)

Blaine, Marge. *The Terrible Thing That Happened at Our House*. New York: Scholastic, 1975. (When Mother finds it necessary to return to work as a science teacher, the entire family suffers the stress which can result when both parents work.

Burton, Virginia L. *Katy and the Big Snow*. Boston: Houghton Mifflin, 1943. (A small town is paralyzed by a huge snowstorm until Katy can plow the streets and people can resume offering their services to the community.)

_____. *Mike Mulligan and His Steam Shovel*. Boston: Houghton Mifflin, 1939. (Modern technology condemns a worthy steam shovel to the junk heap, until Mike finds a way to prove her continued value to society.)

_____. *The Little House*. Boston: Houghton Mifflin, 1942. (As the city expands, the little house is surrounded by buildings, highways, noise, pollution, and other problems of urban growth.)

Coerr, Eleanor. *The Big Balloon Race*. New York: Harper and Row, 1981. (Late nineteenth-century society and transportation technology are portrayed in this story of an actual event.)

Cole, Joanna. *The Magic School Bus at the Waterworks*. New York: Scholastic, 1986. (The water cycle and the process of providing clean water are detailed on a magical trip through the waterworks.)

_____. *The Magic Schoolbus inside the Earth*. New York: Scholastic, 1988. (The geological structure and composition of the earth is seen by students who realize how minerals and rocks from inside the earth are necessary to their lives.)

Delton, Judith, and Ruth Tucker. *My Grandmother's in a Nursing Home*. Niles, Ill.: Albert Whitman, 1986. (His grandmother's Alzheimer's disease prevents her from remembering his name, but a small boy realizes how important his visits are to her and the other patients.)

DePaola, Tomie. *Michael Bird-Boy*. Englewood Cliffs, N.J.: Prentice-Hall, 1975. (A black cloud of pollution threatens the environment of a small boy, who sets out to find its cause and offer a solution.)

_____. *Nana Upstairs, Nana Downstairs*. New York: Penguin Books, 1973. (Grandmother lived downstairs and helped care for great grandmother who lived upstairs. A visit there was always a double treat for this young boy.)

_____. *Now One Foot, Now the Other*. New York: G. P. Putnam's Sons, 1981. (As Bobby helps his grandfather recover from a stroke, we realize the problems of the elderly and the role of medical advances of our society.)

Gag, Wanda. *Millions of Cats*. New York: Coward-McCann, 1928. (Millions of cats can lead to many societal problems, including overpopulation, depleting of water and land resources, and ultimately to conflict. Is isolationism the answer?)

Geisel, Theodore Seuss. (Dr. Seuss.) *The Butter Battle Book*. New York: Random House, 1984. (A simple difference of opinion can lead to an arms race for more effective and devastating weapons.)

_____. *The Lorax*. New York: Random House, 1971. (Humanity's needs for manufactured items produces larger and larger factories, which in turn must be supplied by the natural resources of the area.)

Hartford, John. *Steamboat in a Cornfield*. New York: Crown Publishers, 1986. (The steamboat was a symbol of advancing technology in transportation, but even the great steamer "Virginia" was humbled by the forces of nature.)

Hendershot, Judith. *In Coal Country*. New York: Alfred A. Knopf, 1987. (The everyday life of people in a small coal mining community of the 1930s is seen through the eyes of a little girl who was raised there.)

Krause, Robert. *Another Mouse to Feed*. Englewood Cliffs, N.J.: Prentice-Hall, 1987. (The Mouse family takes in another "child" and finds how difficult it is to provide enough food for everyone. Overpopulation and limited resources are a problem.)

Maruki, Toshi. *Hiroshima No Pika*. New York: Lothrop, Lee and Shepard, 1980. (Horrors of the nuclear bombings of Japan in 1945 are told by a little girl who "survived" the event.)

Owens, Mary Beth. *A Caribou Alphabet*. Brunswick, Maine: Dog Ear Press, 1988. (Inspired by a project to ward off extinction of the caribou, this book shows the interdependence of animals and nature, and ultimately, of humans.)

Peet, Bill. *The Wump World*. Boston: Houghton Mifflin, 1970. (Man and machines take a simple grazing environment and turn it into a polluted, industrial complex. After the resources have been consumed, the Pollutians leave to seek a new home and the Wumps emerge from hiding.)

Provensen, Alice, and Martin Provensen. *The Glorious Flight*. New York: Puffin Books, 1983. (Advances in transportation and communication make our present society very different from this nineteenth-century scene.)

Rylant, Cynthia. *When I Was Young in the Mountains*. New York: E. P. Dutton, 1982. (A child remembers the coal mining society of her grandparents and how it affected her own life.)

Sharmat, Mitchell. *Gregory the Terrible Eater*. New York: Four Winds Press, 1980. (The necessity of a proper diet and the problem of solid waste are both evident in this reverse tale of "junk food.")

Silverstein, Shel. *The Giving Tree*. New York: Harper and Row, 1968. (A tree serves many useful purposes for a little boy, but is ultimately destroyed to fulfill his needs as a man.)

Steig, William. *Rotten Island*. Boston: David R. Godine, 1984. (Rotten Island was the epitome of overpopulation, poor land use, hatred, warfare, etc. Could these creatures be saved or was their destruction the only answer?)

Steiner, Jorg. *The Bear Who Wanted to Be a Bear*. New York: Atheneum, 1976. (A forest environment is transformed to an industrial installation, and an unsuspecting bear suddenly is forced into the role of a factory worker, despite protests that he is truly a bear.)

Mayer, Mercer. *The Pied Piper of Hamlin*. New York: Macmillan Publishing, 1987. (The problem of solid waste disposal, disease, and environmental relationships are an important aspect of this familiar tale.)

Willard, Nancy. *The Voyage of the Ludgate Hill*. San Diego, Calif.: Harcourt Brace Jovanovich, 1987. (Advances in ocean transportation are portrayed through the words of Robert Louis Stevenson who crossed the Atlantic without the benefits of modern cruise ships—refrigeration, stabilizers, etc.)

Williams, Margery. *The Velveteen Rabbit*. New York: Alfred A. Knopf, 1984. (This classic story indicates the advances of modern medicine in understanding the causes of illness and the containment of its spread.)

Zemach, Margot. *The Little Red Hen*. New York: Farrar, Straus and Giroux, 1983. (This old tale can be seen as a story of land use and farm production. Is it necessary for everyone to engage in agriculture in order to eat, or should this be the specialty of a few?)

Ziefert, Harriet. *A New Coat for Anna*. New York: Alfred A. Knopf, 1986. (Europe had been devastated by World War II, and everyday necessities were often non-existent. This book traces the age-old method of making a coat through steps such as shearing the sheep, spinning and weaving the cloth, and tailoring the garment.)

Zion, Gene. *Dear Garbage Man*. New York: Harper, 1957. ("One person's trash is another person's treasure" is personified by these children who try to salvage all the "junk" they can from the streets of a big city.)

Zolotow, Charlotte. *I Know an Old Lady*. New York: Greenwillow, 1984. (Growing old has never dampened this lady's zest for life.)

Additional Children's Literature Books Suitable for Developing Integrated Instructional Units

Aardema, Verna. *Why Mosquitoes Buzz in People's Ears*. New York: Dial Books, 1975. (A mosquito is brought to trial for bothering both people and animals.)

Alexander, Lloyd. *The King's Fountain*. New York: E. P. Dutton and Co., 1971. (A rich king wants to build a gorgeous fountain which will cut off the water supply to his subjects. Eventually a poor man convinces him of the folly of his idea.)

Barrett, Judi. *Animals Should Definitely Not Wear Clothing*. New York: Atheneum, 1984. (Adaptation of animals to a different environment can be humorous and educational.)

Barrett, Judi, and Ron Barrett. *Cloudy with a Chance of Meatballs*. New York: Macmillan, 1978. (Everything you need to conceptualize about weather is told in this analogous tale where precipitation from the sky falls in the form of food.)

Briggs, Raymond. *Jim and the Beanstalk*. New York: Coward, McCann and Geoghegan, 1970. (The giant is not so mean after all. He just needs a trip to the oculist, the dentist, and the wigmaker.)

Brown, Marc. *Arthur's Eyes*. Boston: Little, Brown and Co., 1979. (Arthur is teased when he gets glasses, but he soon sees them as a source of pride.)

_____. *Arthur's Nose*. Boston: Little, Brown and Co., 1976. (Unhappy with his nose, Arthur visits the rhinologist to get a new one.)

Burningham, John. *Mr. Gumpy's Outing*. New York: Henry Holt and Co., 1970. (Squabbling animals upset the balance of the boat and everyone must swim to safety.)

Buscaglia, Leo. *The Fall of Freddie the Leaf*. New York: Holt, Rinehart and Winston, 1982. (Falling leaves illustrate the delicate balance between life and death.)

Carle, Eric. *The Mixed Up Chameleon*. New York: Thomas Crowell, 1975. (A very bored chameleon wants to be like other animals, but when he is transformed, he no longer can survive.)

_____. *The Very Busy Spider*. New York: G. P. Putnam, 1984. (A fun way to learn about spiders' activities.)

_____. *The Very Hungry Caterpillar*. New York: Putnam, Philomel Books, 1981. (No self-respecting caterpillar would eat like this, but the process of metamorphosis is integral to their lives.)

Carrick, Carol. *Patrick's Dinosaur*. New York: Houghton Mifflin, 1983. (Patrick is afraid of dinosaurs, until his brother assures him they became extinct millions of years ago.)

Cooney, Barbara. *Island Boy*. New York: Viking Penguin, 1988. (The history of one family's life on an island off New England gives evidence for their self-sufficiency, as well as the need to use and respect nature.)

_____. *Miss Rumphius*. New York: Viking Penguin, 1982. (In her world travels, Miss Rumphius realizes how landforms and climate influence everyone's lives, but she's happiest on her little island by the sea.)

DePaola, Tomie. *The Popcorn Book*. New York: Holiday House, 1978. (There is a lot to learn about popcorn besides how good it tastes.)

_____. *The Quicksand Book*. New York. Holiday House, 1977. (Everything you ever wanted to know about quicksand and how to escape it.)

Ekker, Ernst. *What Is beyond the Hill?* New York: J. B. Lippincott, 1985. (Infinity is forever.)

Gobel, Paul. *The Girl Who Loved Wild Horses*. New York: Macmillan Publishing, 1978. (The life of a Plains Indian girl establishes the interdependence of man, nature, and the total environment.)

Hader, Berta, and Elmer Hader. *The Big Snow*. New York: Macmillan, 1948. (A snowstorm alters the forest environment.)

Keats, Ezra Jack. *The Snowy Day*. New York: Viking Press, 1962. (Peter delights in the qualities of the snow.)

Krauss, Ruth. *The Carrot Seed*. New York: Harper and Row, 1945. (Seeds can be sprouted under various conditions.)

Lionni, Leo. *The Biggest House in the World*. New York: Pantheon, 1970. (A snail who wants a bigger house hears the story of another snail with similar desires and the catastrophe that resulted.)

_____. *Fish Is Fish*. New York: Pantheon, 1970. (A tadpole turns into a frog and goes out into the world. Later when he returns to the pond he tells a minnow of the various creatures while the minnow imagines them each as modifications of his own body.)

_____. *Frederick's Fables*. New York: Random House, 1985. (A collection of thirteen Lionni stories, nearly all of them suitable for science lessons.)

Lobel, Arnold. *Grasshopper on the Road*. New York: Harper and Row, 1978. (Grasshopper's journey introduces us to the world of insects.)

MacDonald, Golden. *The Little Island*. Garden City, N.Y.: Doubleday and Co., 1946. (The ecologies of the land, sea, and air interact on this small, nearly deserted island.)

McCloskey, Robert. *Blueberries for Sal*. New York: Viking Press, 1948. (Human beings and wild animals live strangely parallel lives.)

_____. *Burt Dow Deep-Water Man*. New York: Viking Press, 1963. (A merchant seaman retires to the Maine coast which leads to adventures with a pod of whales.)

_____. *One Morning in Maine*. New York: Viking Press, 1952. (The Maine coast is the background for a day in the life of an adventurous little girl.)

Miles, Miska. *Small Rabbit*. New York: Scholastic, 1977. (A rabbit must learn to avoid its predators.)

Miller, Edna. *Mousekin Finds a Friend*. Englewood Cliffs, N.J.: Prentice-Hall, 1967. (A panorama of the forest environment helps compare and contrast the animals and plants which live there. The predator-prey relationship and the food chain are shown.)

_____. *Mousekin Takes a Trip*. Englewood Cliffs, N.J.: Prentice-Hall, 1976. (The desert environment is seen through the eyes of a small mouse in this fantasy story.)

_____. *Mousekin's Woodland Birthday Party*. Englewood Cliffs, N.J.: 1974. (The life cycle of the mouse is excellently detailed from conception throughout life. Also published as *Mousekin's Birth*.)

Oakley, Graham. *The Church Mice and the Moon*. London: Macmillan Children's Books, 1974. (Scientists launch a rocket with mice on board—so they think.)

Politi, Leo. *Song of the Swallows*. New York: Charles Scribner's Sons, 1949. (A small boy in San Juan Capistrano learns about the swallows from an old mission worker.)

Pollock, Penny. *The Slug Who Thought He Was a Snail*. New York: G. P. Putnam's Sons, 1980. (The slug thinks he has lost his house and goes off to look for it. Finally another slug tells him the truth.)

Salten, Felix. *Bambi*. New York: Simon and Schuster, 1928. (This is the original children's classic, not the Disney version of the famous deer story.)

Selsam, Millicent. *Terry and the Caterpillars*. New York: Harper and Row, 1962. (All about caterpillars and life cycles.)

Shaw, Charles. *It Looked Like Spilled Milk*. New York: Harper and Row, 1947. (Rorschach-type splotches look like various items but turn out to be a cloud.)

Steig, William. *Amos and Boris*. New York: Puffin Books, 1977. (A tiny mouse and a huge whale find friendship after doing each other a favor.)

Ungerer, Tomi. *Moon Man*. New York: Harper and Row, 1967. (What would happen if the man in the moon could pay a visit to the earth for one day?)

Van Allsburg, Chris. *The Wreck of the Zephyr*. New York: Houghton Mifflin, 1983. (A visitor hears a mystical story of sailing.)

Walter, Mildred Pitts. *Ty's One Man Band*. New York: Scholastic, 1980. (The study of sound as produced by primitive instruments as well as the human voice is essential to this story of the rural South.)

Ward, Lynn. *The Biggest Bear*. Boston: Houghton Mifflin, 1952. (A young boy tries to raise a bear cub, to the dismay of the entire household.)

Yolen, Jane. *All in the Woodland Early*. Cleveland, Ohio: William Collins, 1979. (Rhythm and rhyme help teach the names of North American birds, animals, and insects. A song is included.)

INTRODUCTION TO
PARTS 2, 3, AND 4

The remainder of *Teaching Science through Children's Literature: An Integrated Approach* provides activities for teachers to consider for use in the classroom. Thirty-three children's books which are easily adapted to the integration of science, language arts, and other areas of the curriculum have been selected. They are divided into the three major categories of science—life science, earth and space science, and physical science, to coincide with the divisions of well-known science projects and text series.

Within each division, books which are easier to read and conceptually less complex are listed first. These may be most beneficial in lower grades. The ensuing books are more difficult and may be of more use in the middle and upper elementary grades. However, many of these books can be used in any integrated classroom K-6, depending on the objectives which the teacher has determined for the unit, and the particular activities selected for the lesson.

Each set of activities is basically written for children to perform under the supervision or facilitation of the teacher or other adult. However, it is the prerogative of each individual teacher to decide if the activity would best be carried out as a whole class activity, in small groups, or by individuals. In many cases, such as corresponding with organizations, collecting specimens, gathering equipment, or choosing supplemental trade books for silent reading time, the teacher must be in charge of the process to have materials accessible for classroom work. However, it is desirable and most effective if the children are given the major responsibility for carrying out the tasks and not acting as spectators.

The number of activities provided for any one book far exceeds the amount of time which could be allotted to a single topic. The teacher must choose which activities best suit the classroom situation and available resources. Also, these may be used in conjunction with a text series, which would help delineate the activities which would best correspond to the objectives of the school curriculum. Another major point to remember in selecting items is to choose a variety of activities which reflect the different content areas of the curriculum and various comprehension strategies (e.g., inferences, predictions, comparisons) as well as the basic language arts areas—reading, writing, speaking, and listening.

Books and references related to the activities are listed at the end of the appropriate activity. Specific recordings of songs and music are offered only as examples of what was available to the authors at the time of this writing—they do not constitute recommendations of certain recordings over others.

Part II
LIFE SCIENCE

3

TREES

A Tree Is Nice

Janice Udry
New York: Harper and Row, 1956

Summary

Living trees are very important to people and animals. They provide many items we need and are sources of comfort and recreation.

Science Topic Areas

Uses of trees, parts and kinds of trees, tree growth, planting techniques

Content Related Words

Leaves, trunk, roots

Activities

1. The teacher and children can make a chart or concept map showing the uses of trees, e.g., recreation, food, building, etc. Do this for human and animal needs.

2. Botanists refer to trees as coniferous or deciduous. What does this mean? Which ones are more common where the children live? Gather fallen pieces from both kinds of trees and make a display.

3. As a class, write a letter to the state forest service asking for written materials on trees in your state. Be sure to use correct letter writing form. Use this information for displays or as an information source as you do this unit.

4. Collect and be able to recognize leaves from five different trees native to your area. Perhaps this can be done during a nature walk near your school.

5. Be able to recognize the bark of five different trees indigenous to your area. Try not to select five varieties of maple, five evergreens, etc. In winter, leaf identification cannot be used so other methods should be known.

6. Find a forested area, if possible, and label a section of trees by variety. Do similar trees tend to exist in groups or are they mixed randomly? Measure the circumference of the trees and determine which kinds are the largest and the smallest. Look for full-grown trees, not saplings.

7. Gather seeds from various types of trees. How are they protected on the tree and after they fall? How are they transported in nature?

8. Using a catalog from a nursery, decide which species of tree would be best to plant in your school yard. Consider growth rate, climatic needs, etc. Raise money or have a parent group help you purchase the tree. Consult a gardening book or other set of directions to be sure you plant it properly. Assign students to water and care for the tree.

9. If you live in a city, have a tree in your classroom, e.g., a Norfolk Island pine. What care must it be given? Where else do you see trees in a city—parks, shopping malls, etc. What kind are they? Why do people want trees in these settings?

10. Measure the temperature in the shade of a tree and in bright sunlight. Do this at various times of the day for a week. Make a chart or graph for each and compare.

11. Find pictures of trees that are unique to certain areas, e.g., the Joshua tree of southern California or the cypress tree of the Monterey peninsula. Why do some trees grow only in certain areas?

12. What are the characteristics that distinguish a tree during the four seasons? Make drawings or collect pictures of trees at different times of the year. Which trees change the most in the fall? Which change the least? Which are most common to the area where you live?

13. Look at a tree stump or a piece of firewood to see the growth rings of the tree. How old was the tree if each ring equals a year? (See figure 3.1.)

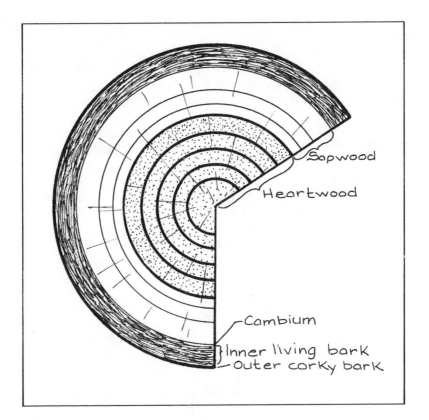

Fig. 3.1. A Tree Cross Section Showing Growth Rings.

14. The tree has a yearly life cycle. The teacher could read to the class *The Fall of Freddie the Leaf* by Leo Buscaglia. Why do Freddie and Daniel turn color? Why must they "fall"? How does this story relate to human beings and their life?

15. A tree that is diseased or not growing properly must be treated or it will die. Consult the yellow pages of the phone book for a tree service or a county extension agent who can provide help. What type of treatments might be recommended?

16. Your town has a street lined with huge old oak trees. Officials feel these must be cut down so that the street can be widened to allow more traffic. Write a letter voicing your opinions or have a debate with people representing different sides of the issue. Give reasons. Don't just get emotional.

17. What are the ways trees have been important in history or to people in class—boundary markers, meeting places, e.g., Robin Hood's oak tree. Why do you think this is so?

18. What is the most important thing about living trees for you personally? Write an essay to share your thoughts.

19. Make masks or paper bag costumes to represent the parts of a tree—root, bark, branch, leaf, bud, etc. Present a short speech on how important they are to the life of the whole tree, or be interviewed by another student.

20. You have been selected to head a new advertising campaign for the U.S. Forest Service. You must write three TV commercials for Smokey the Bear and design a bumper sticker concerning safety with fire in the woods.

21. Put some twigs from trees in water in the spring and watch them sprout. Flowering trees and willows work well.

22. Make a forest collage using only silhouettes of trees (see figure 3.2). Tissue paper allows you to overlap colors and produce new shades to give the effect of the autumn color change.

Fig. 3.2. Shapes of Common Trees.

23. Use trees for art projects such as twig mobiles or bark and leaf rubbings. (Leaf rubbings work best if the vein side of the leaf is next to the paper. Using the side of a crayon gives a more even impression.) For apple prints, cut the fruit in half crosswise, dip into ink and press on paper like a stamp pad.

24. Many poems have been written about trees or forests. You can write one, perhaps in the form of a tree. A triangular-shaped poem can help express holiday greetings.

25. In the biography section of the library media resource center, look for books on Johnny Appleseed (Jonathan Chapman) and John Muir. Dramatize a scene from the life of these persons. How were they important to the "tree population" of this country?

26. Read *The Giving Tree* by Shel Silverstein. What is your opinion of the boy in the story? Is the use of trees the same in both books?

27. Listen to music written about trees, e.g., *The Pines of Rome* by Ottorino Respighi.

Related Books and References

Buscaglia, Leo. *The Fall of Freddie the Leaf*. Holt, Rinehart and Winston, 1982.

Respighi, Ottorino. *The Pines of Rome*. (E.g., The New York Philharmonic, Leonard Bernstein conducting. Columbia recording.)

Silverstein, Shel. *The Giving Tree*. New York: Harper and Row, 1964.

4

SEEDS

The Tiny Seed
Eric Carle
Natick, Mass.: Picture Book Studio, USA, 1987

Summary

Wind, weather, and water can prevent seeds from taking root and growing. But some seeds still overcome these problems and find the proper conditions to flourish and bloom.

Science Topic Areas

Seed distribution, conditions favorable to germination and growth, life cycle of a flowering plant

Content Related Words

Seed, dispersal, roots, stems, leaves

Activities

1. Stuff an old sock or nylon stocking with crumpled paper and tie it shut with a yard of heavy string. Drag this through a field or along the forest floor. The sock will pick up seeds, which can be taken back to class for examination. An alternate method for gathering seeds is to spread a sheet under a tree and gently shake the tree. Ripe seeds will fall onto the sheet.

2. Observe seeds under a microscope or with a hand lens. Use seeds you have gathered outdoors, packaged flower or vegetable seeds, or seeds from fresh fruits and vegetables, e.g., tomatoes, snap beans, kiwis, oranges. Write descriptions of the seeds so that others can identify the seeds from what you have written.

3. Collect seeds found in the fall—burdocks, milkweeds, thistles. After you study the dried plant, the seed pod and stalk can be spray painted and used for a fall "flower" arrangement.

4. Seeds are dispersed or carried by various means—water, wind, animals. They are made so that they can float, glide, shoot into the air, or catch onto animals and people. Take a few dried beans and invent a new seed by attaching art scraps, cotton, packing materials, etc., to the seed. Write an adventure story about the seed and integrate a description of the seed dispersal method used.

5. Make a list of edible seeds and bring in samples, e.g., sunflower, sesame, pumpkin, poppy seeds. Many spices are seeds that are used whole or ground to powder. A display of these can be made by placing several seeds or the ground spice onto lengths of wide transparent tape, which can then be attached to posterboard and labeled.

6. Make a quick, easy snack that requires no baking.

Crunchy Seed Candy

Mix together the following ingredients:

1 cup sunflower seeds
1 cup honey
1 cup peanut butter
1 cup cocoa powder

Shape into one inch balls.
Spread one cup of sesame seeds on a sheet of waxed paper.
Roll each piece of candy in sesame seeds.

7. Sprouted seeds are tasty additions to salads and other foods, and are a good source of protein. Use beans, lentils, alfalfa, wheat, mung, barley, or soy seeds. Place about one tablespoon of seeds in a clean glass jar. Cover the top with a piece of clean nylon stocking or several layers of nylon net held in place with a rubber band. Soak the seeds in warm water overnight. Drain and rinse them through the material. Each morning and evening run fresh warm water on the seeds and drain them. Sprouts should appear in a few days. (See figure 4.1.)

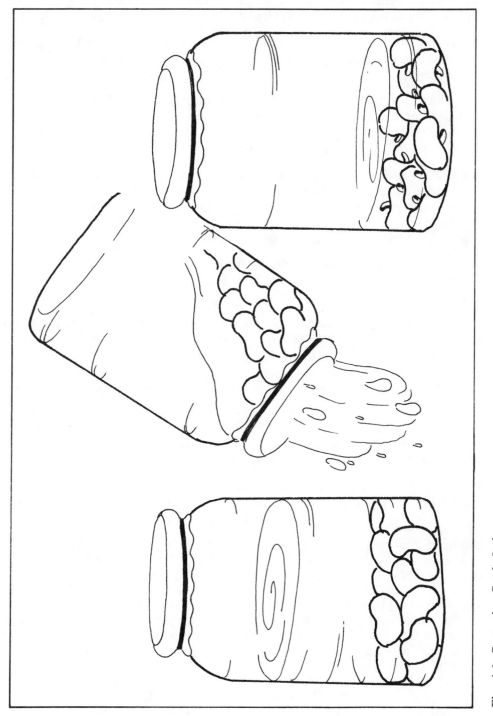

Fig. 4.1. Sprouting Seeds Indoors.

8. Soak dried beans overnight in water. Break them open gently and look for the embryonic plant in the middle. The two halves contain stored food for plant growth.

9. Birdseed placed on a moist sponge will also sprout. How many kinds of plants do you observe? Keep the sponge in a shallow dish and add water to the dish so as not to disturb the sprouts.

10. Grow fast-sprouting seeds (radish, carrot, mustard) in different media, i.e., soil, vermiculite, sand, clay. Alter the growing conditions—amount of sunlight, moisture, kind of water (tap, distilled, water with a bit of vinegar or lime added). Keep a daily log or sketches to show changes in the plants.

11. Some seeds and plants are poisonous. Garden fertilizers and plant food can also be very dangerous. Find out which poisonous plants are common in your area or are around the house, e.g., poinsettias. What steps should you take if you think a small child has eaten something poisonous? Check the phone book for a Poison Control Center and learn what kind of information and services they provide.

12. Decorate sticky labels with plants or flowers and put down the phone number of the Poison Control Center or other information agency near you. These can be put on home phones or on the cover of the phone book.

13. You have been given a seed catalog and asked to choose five varieties of flowers for a small garden (5' x 5') at the entrance of the school. You should select flowers that all grow under the same natural conditions and will present a variety of heights. You may wish to have them all the same color or coordinated shades. How many flowers or seed packs will you need? How much will it cost? After your selection, learn to fill out the order blank and envelope.

14. What basic gardening tools would you need to plant this small garden and keep it watered? Look in a newspaper ad or catalog from a hardware or garden supply store. Make a list and decide how much it will cost.

15. Read the back of a flower or vegetable seed package. What can you learn about this plant from the information given there? Compare this information with an entry in a garden encyclopedia. Which is more complete and helpful?

16. Dig up clumps of several different weeds, leaving the roots intact. Mask the roots with bags so students can guess what the root will look like after seeing the plant. How do roots differ from one another? What is the job of the root?

17. The stem of a flower or plant carries water and food to the flower and leaves. This can be demonstrated by setting a stalk of celery in a jar of ink or colored water. Another method is to use a white carnation. Slit the stem lengthwise. Stand one section in plain water and the other in water tinted with food coloring. What color will the carnation be in a few hours?

18. Raise some houseplants in the classroom. Select both flowering and foliage types. Make a "care card" to accompany each plant, e.g., amount of sunlight and water needed, special fertilizer requirements. How can you tell if the plant is getting improper care, has become infested with a disease, needs to be repotted, etc.? What steps must be taken to cure these problems?

19. An avocado seed will often grow into a large houseplant. Wash the seed in bleach, then rinse and dry it thoroughly. Stick toothpicks into the seed at three different spots about one-third of the distance up from the pointed end. Suspend the seed in a cup of water with the toothpicks resting on the edge of the cup. (See figure 4.2.) Change water regularly. Place the rooted seed in a 6-inch flower pot which is partially filled with good potting soil. Add enough soil to barely cover the seed and press the soil down gently. Continue to water as needed. Try the same activity using a potato that has well-developed "eyes."

Fig. 4.2. Rooting an Avocado Seed.

20. Look up florists in the phone book. Check the special services they offer, e.g., flowers by wire, church arrangements, dried flowers, balloons. Make a chart comparing the different stores.

21. Do the same for gardening supply shops or nurseries.

22. Write a poem, couplet, or description about a flower, seed, or plant. You can be very serious or this might be a chance to show your humor.

23. Make seed pictures or ornaments. Spread white glue thinly on a cardboard cutout, then arrange various seeds (dried peas, beans, lentils, peppercorns, sunflowers, pumpkins, etc.), to make an abstract design or actual scene. Seeds should be only one layer thick and can be sprayed with clear art varnish or painted with diluted white glue to keep them in place and add lustre.

24. Learn songs about flowers or plants, e.g., "Edelweiss" from *The Sound of Music* by Rodgers and Hammerstein.

25. Take a tune you know and write your own words about a plant or flower. Can you make up rhymes about dandelions? crabgrass? a cactus plant?

26. Read some legends or folklore about plants or flowers, e.g., *The Legend of the Bluebonnet* by Tomie dePaola.

27. Look in the *Farmer's Almanac* or *Bartlett's Familiar Quotations* for famous sayings about plants or flowers. Put these on large cards and use them as part of displays or artwork done during this unit. Perhaps the library media specialist could set up a display of books on plants, flowers, gardening, etc., and include your cards and artwork.

28. Make paper flowers and leaves. Choose a flower that exists or invent your own species. Use paper cutouts, origami, etc.

29. Tissue-paper flowers can be made by cutting out six or eight circles, 6 inches in diameter. Place a pencil in the middle of the sheets, eraser end down. Gather up the sheets and tie a string or wind a wire around the pencil about half an inch from the end of the eraser. Remove the pencil and pull the string or wire tight. Wire or pipe cleaner stems and cut-out leaves can be added.

Related Books and References

DePaola, Tomie. *The Legend of the Bluebonnet*. New York: Putnam, 1983.

Kraus, Ruth. *The Carrot Seed*. New York: Harper and Row, 1945.

Rodgers, Richard, and Oscar Hammerstein II. *The Sound of Music*. Movie soundtrack. RCA Victor recording.

Sakata, Hideaki. *Origami*. New York: Harper and Row, 1986.

5

ANIMAL REPRODUCTION AND DEVELOPMENT

Mousekin's Birth

Edna Miller
Englewood Cliffs, N.J.: Prentice-Hall, 1974
(Originally titled *Mousekin's Woodland Birthday*)

Summary

From the moment of conception until his first efforts to view the wonders of the world, Mousekin's development is traced in words and sketches. Gestation, birth, and postnatal care for mammals is contrasted with that for other classes of animals.

Science Topic Areas

Reproduction, embryo genesis and development, animal birth, characteristics of mammals, postnatal care

Content Related Words

Reproduction, cell, embryo, teat, sperm, egg, fertile, nourish, womb

Activities

1. Identify all the animals shown in the book. Put them in categories—mammals, reptiles, fish, amphibians. Find pictures of these creatures for a wall display. What additional common animals could be placed in each category? You will need to know the characteristics of each group to do this. (See figure 5.1.)

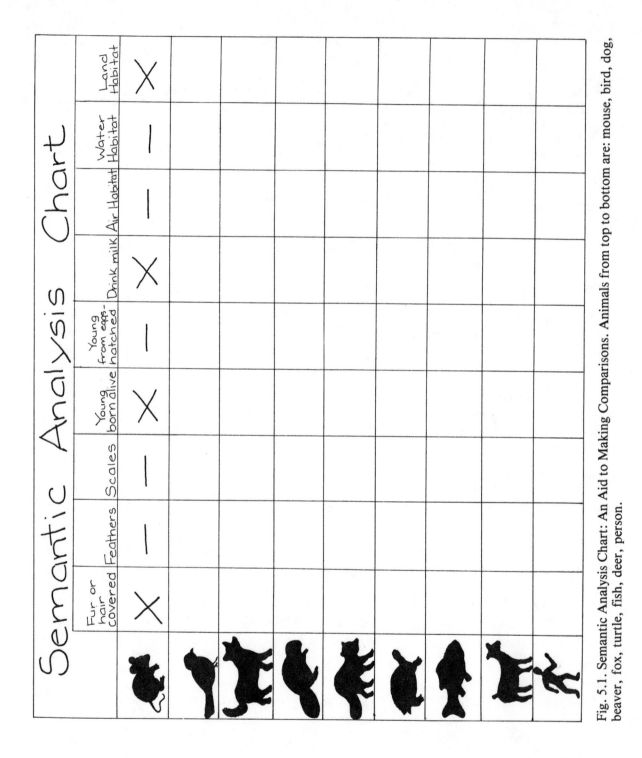

Fig. 5.1. Semantic Analysis Chart: An Aid to Making Comparisons. Animals from top to bottom are: mouse, bird, dog, beaver, fox, turtle, fish, deer, person.

2. Set up small groups of students and assign each one an animal from your display. For each animal look up (a) gestation period for babies, (b) size when born, (c) expected adult size, and (d) any unique characteristics at time of birth or shortly after, e.g., can walk immediately, born blind, etc. Be sure to include human babies. Have the library media specialist help you locate nonfictional books on animal babies. Many nature magazines for young children feature excellent articles on this. Perhaps these are also available.

3. Have a representative of each group line up, starting with the animal having the shortest gestation period going to the animal with the longest. Next, sequence the animals according to birth size—smallest to largest. Next, put them in order according to anticipated adult size. Keep a list of the order on the board. Do the children stay in the same places? Which animals seem to change places the most?

4. What are the characteristics of a mammal? Identify some well-known and lesser-known mammals and let each child adopt one to look up. Have them report on their animals' more unusual features.

5. What is the role of the egg in the reproductive cycle? Get some frog eggs from a pond or stagnant stream and raise them in the classroom. What environment and food source is necessary to maintain life? Draw and/or describe the stages of growth. Later the animal could be measured or weighed. (Check a book on amphibians for information.)

6. Obtain some fish eggs (caviar). Examine them with a hand lens. How does the size, shape, and other features compare to bird or chicken eggs? To the egg of a mammal?

7. Gerbils are also good animals to raise in the classroom. It is very possible there will be babies if you have a male and a female.

8. Compare the number of babies that each animal in the book has. Multiple births are less common for humans. What do you call two babies born at the same time? three babies?, etc. Do any students in the class represent these groups? Are they identical in looks?

9. Study a diagram or plastic model of a fetus in the womb. What features do you notice? Why is there an umbilical cord? What must happen to the fetus before it is ready to be born?

10. Interview a teacher or parent who is expecting a baby. Can she share some of the experiences of her pregnancy or answer questions from the students? Has she had any of the tests, such as sonograms, that give parents much information on their baby before it is born?

11. Some human babies receive nourishment from their mothers after birth, while some take milk from a bottle. Get folders from a pediatrician explaining these two methods of feeding. What eating schedule do infants need? Read the labels from several different brands of baby formula. What are the ingredients? Are the brands similar? How should bottles and formulas be prepared for a baby?

12. Animal parents need to have a nest or other safe habitat in which to have their babies. What materials do they use to build nests?

13. Survey the class to see where they were born. On a large map, indicate the city and date of birth of each class member. How many states are represented? Any foreign countries? Were children born in hospitals, at home, or elsewhere?

14. Parents usually buy many items before their baby is born. Make a checklist of necessities, e.g., crib, diapers, etc. Use a catalog from a department or discount store to list these items and total the cost. What items would need to be purchased in another kind of store and what price would they be? (The items need not include clothes and toys.) This could be done in small groups or as a class. Does "necessity" mean the same to everyone?

15. Human babies develop very slowly compared to most other creatures. It is many months before they begin to have teeth. Try making some teething biscuits. Why are these given to babies?

Teething Biscuits

Beat 2 eggs until creamy.
Add one scant cup of sugar and stir with eggs.
Gradually add 2 to 2½ cups flour until dough is stiff.
Roll out between sheets of floured wax paper to ¾-inch thickness.
Cut into shapes and let stand overnight on a greased cookie sheet.
Bake at 325 degrees until browned.
Makes one dozen biscuits.

16. Bring in baby photos (teacher included) and make an anonymous display. Try to match these to present school photos after the identities are guessed.

17. If you can obtain the figures, bring in your height and weight at birth, when you started school, and at the present time. Rank order each set of figures for the class, so there are three columns for height and three for weight. Compare where your name lies and make a line graph for your height and your weight. You can compare your own figures to a height and weight chart found in the *World Almanac*, but remember these figures are averages and individual cases can vary considerably.

18. Invite parents of students to bring in baby brothers or sisters, preferably ones under a year old. What can babies do at these ages? Notice their ability to move, communicate, express emotion and desires, etc. Write out the observations you made and also tell what impressed you most about the baby (babies).

19. What are some things you must know about holding or handling a baby? Contrast this to the way Mousekin was carried by his mother—with her teeth. Investigate how other animals transport their babies. What various ways do humans use?

20. Why are pets and other animals able to perform tasks so much sooner than human babies?

21. Parents often sing lullabies to babies to help them go to sleep. Do you remember any that were sung to you? Many songs originated from other countries, e.g., Brahm's "Lullaby" is German, "All through the Night" is Welsh, "Hush, Little Baby" is English. Have the library media specialist help you find lullabies from your country of origin.

22. Adoption is an important part of the lives of many children. Read and discuss books on this topic, e.g., *Abby*.

Related Books and References

Caines, Jeannette. *Abby*. New York: Harper and Row, 1974.

Clifton, Lucille. *Everett Anderson's Nine Month Long*. New York: Holt, 1988.

Horne, Marilyn, and Richard Robinson. *Lullabies from 'round the World*. (A sound recording.) Rhythm Productions, P.O. Box 34485, Whitney Boulevard, Los Angeles, CA 90034.

Wilder, Alec, and Maurice Sendak. *Lullabies and Night Songs*. New York: Harper and Row, 1965.

Yolen, Jane. *Lullaby Songbook*. New York: Harcourt Brace Jovanovich, 1986.

6

DUCKS AND OTHER BIRDS

Make Way for Ducklings
Robert McCloskey
New York: The Viking Press, 1941

Summary

Mr. and Mrs. Mallard find that the proper environment for raising their ducklings can be in the middle of a crowded city. Despite the obstacles involved, Boston's Public Gardens is a suitable habitat for these wild ducks.

Science Topic Areas

Ducks (birds, in general), physical characteristics, behavior, habitat, survival instinct, reproductive instinct

Content Related Words

Instinct, habitat, environment, waddle, predator

Activities

1. Hatch baby ducklings in the class. This involves obtaining fertilized eggs, having someone supervise the project, making arrangements for someone to raise the ducks, and checking the regulations of doing this in the classroom. (A local agricultural extension agent might help.)

2. Keep a daily log or series of sketches throughout this process. Compare what you see with the inside flyleaf of the book, which shows the stages of an egg hatching.

3. Examine a feather with a hand lens or microscope. What do you observe? Are all the feathers on a duck identical in size, color, texture, purpose? What is the reason for this?

4. Look in a field guide on ducks. What colors are mallards? Are males and females the same? Why or why not? Make colored drawings of the adult ducks. Note that the male has more coloration lines. (See figure 6.1.)

Fig. 6.1. Color Us: Mr. and Mrs. Mallard.

5. Ducks are colored white on their undersides so they cannot be seen by predators in the water as they swim. To show this, paint potatoes a variety of colors or cut circles from an array of colored papers. Hang these from the ceiling or overhead hooks. If you were the predator, which would be the easiest to see, the hardest to see?

6. What color are mallard duck eggs? Use hard-boiled eggs or plastic nylon stocking containers to reproduce the characteristics of the eggs. Gather materials from your yard or around the school and build a nest for the eggs. Make sure the colors will help hide the eggs from enemies.

7. Locate Boston, Massachusetts on a map of the United States and on a map of Massachusetts. A map of the city of Boston, obtainable from an automobile club or the Chamber of Commerce of Boston, would also be very helpful.

8. On the Boston city map, locate the Commons, the Public Gardens, Beacon Hill, Beacon Street, Louisburg Square, and Mt. Vernon Street. What other bodies of water lie in and around Boston? Locate famous buildings or other places you have learned about in social studies, e.g., Paul Revere's house, the Old North Church, the Boston Tea Party site, *Old Ironsides*, etc. (Small duck-shaped cutouts could be labeled and tacked on the map in the correct positions.)

9. You work for one of the large radio stations in Boston and have heard that a family of ducks is seeking a home. What qualities must the home possess and what type places must be avoided? Write an appeal to the people of Boston to help find a home. Use this as a class presentation to practice your information-gathering and speaking skills.

10. Design a "Duck Crossing" sign to assist Officer Clancy as he directs traffic.

11. Mr. and Mrs. Mallard love Boston so much they write to many of their relatives inviting them to visit. As a group, decide what this letter would contain and write it on a flip chart or poster.

12. Pretend you are other members of the fowl family—chickens, turkeys, swans, geese, pigeons. Look up the major characteristics of these types of fowl and see if their needs would fit into the habitat and lifestyle of the Mallards. Decide whether or not they will accept the Mallards' invitation to visit or must decline, e.g., chickens do not fly well and would have trouble getting there. Write a reply letter. You might do this on duck-shaped paper and display the replies with the original invitation.

13. Many birds migrate for the winter. If this unit is being done during the fall or spring, watch for flocks of birds. What kind are they? In which direction are they flying? How many appear to travel together? Do they all fly in formation? For a couple of weeks, record this information along with the time of day you see the birds. Ask the library media specialist to recommend an atlas or other reference book that would contain a map of common flyways used by birds. Do you live near one of these flyways?

14. Compare the life of the Mallards to the swallows of Capistrano, as shown in *Song of the Swallows*. What instincts help guide the lives of these birds?

15. Learn the characteristics that make birds a unique group of animals. Then work in pairs or small groups to make specific information cards about a variety of birds. Those shown in figure 6.2 are 1) penguin, 2) robin, 3) pigeon, 4) woodpecker, 5) owl, 6) parakeet, 7) hummingbird, 8) parrot, 9) eagle, 10) ostrich. Note the adult size of these birds and put them in order from largest to smallest—e.g. emperor penguins are 4 feet high; parakeets are about 6 inches. Use cash register tape as a visual indicator on a display area—4 feet for the penguin, etc.

Fig. 6.2. Scale Comparisons of Commonly Known Birds.

16. Ducks are characterized by their webbed feet, used as an aid in swimming. How have people used this feature to help propel them in water, both swimming and boating? Bring in examples of these devices, e.g., swim fins, paddles, oars. If you have access to a swimming pool, experiment with these to see how efficiency can be increased.

17. Think of other sets of eight rhyming names that could have been used for the ducklings, e.g., Tim, Slim, Jim, etc.

18. The duck is an important character in the musical story *Peter and the Wolf* by Serge Prokofiev. What instrument represents the duck? Why do you think it was chosen? What other implements are used to imitate the sound of a duck?

19. Wild ducks are often hunted by sportsmen. What are the rules and regulations concerning this in your state, e.g., time and length of season, type of weapon, etc.?

20. What is a bird sanctuary or wildlife refuge? Why do they exist? Who supports and runs them? Locate one near you and learn about it — they are often listed on a state highway or recreation map.

Related Books and References

Carlson, Nancy, trans. *Peter and the Wolf*. New York: Viking Penguin/Puffin Books, 1986.

Flack, Marjorie. *The Story about Ping*. New York: Viking Press, 1933.

Peterson, Roger Tory. *A Field Guide to the Birds*. Boston: Houghton Mifflin, 1947.

Politi, Leo. *Song of the Swallows*. New York: Charles Scribner's Sons, 1949.

Prokofiev, Serge. *Peter and the Wolf*. (E.g., The Boston Pops Orchestra, John Williams conducting. Philips recordings.)

Tafuri, Nancy. *Have You Seen My Duckling?* New York: Greenwillow, 1984.

7

ANTS AND OTHER INSECTS

Two Bad Ants

Chris Van Allsburg
Boston: Houghton Mifflin, 1988

Summary

The quest for a mysterious sweet-tasting crystal leads to near disaster for two curious ants. They persevere to overcome many trials and tribulations of the outside world before returning to the safety of the ant colony.

Science Topic Areas

Insects, the life of an ant, physical and social qualities of the ant world, predator-prey relationships, the ant in the human's world, household safety, magnification, the senses

Content Related Words

Crystal, scout, queen, insect, antennae, colony

Activities

1. On a walk outside, look for ant hills and ant trails. What are dangers for ants as they move about? If there are spider webs handy, look for evidence of spiders feeding on ants.

2. Observe the kinds of food that ants seek in nature.

3. What methods do the ants utilize to transport food back to their home?

4. See how far an ant can walk in a minute.

5. Have a snack outside and see which of your foods attract ants. Include items that represent the four basic tastes—sweet, sour, bitter, and salty.

6. Keep an ant farm in the classroom to study these insects.

7. Observe ants moving on a clear tray which has been placed on the overhead projector. How do they move and react? Create a list of words or phrases to describe their actions.

8. Observe ants with hand lenses or insect boxes, then build an ant using pipe cleaners or modeling clay. The game *Cootie* can help you learn the parts of the ant's body.

9. Look at other familiar objects under the hand lens or microscope. Compare the appearance of bread, onion skins, oatmeal, salt, sand, sugar, tea, and other materials. Write descriptions of how these would appear to an ant.

10. Many objects in nature are made of crystals. You can grow salt or sugar crystals on a string. For salt crystals, put 8 to 10 teaspoons of plain table salt into 1 cup of water and stir until it dissolves. Tie a string around a pencil. Place the pencil across the cup and let it rest there. Submerge the string in the water but do not let the string touch the bottom of the cup. Allow the water to evaporate. Crystals will form on the string. (See figure 7.1.) Observe these through a hand lens or microscope. Draw pictures of the shapes you see. Follow the same procedures for sugar crystals using ½ cup water and 26 level teaspoons of white sugar.

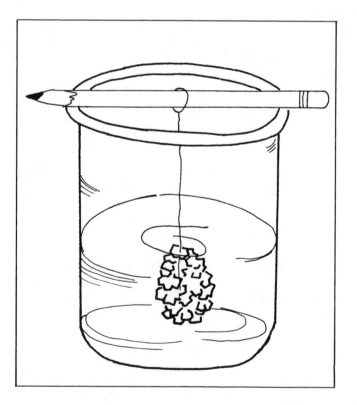

Fig. 7.1. Growing Crystals on a String.

11. Duplicate the paper templates in figure 7.2 for common crystal shapes such as four- or six- or twelve-sided solids. Fold these into the crystal forms and glue the tabs to secure the crystal. Explore the ways the sides appear to change after folding. Make mobiles of completed solids. Compare them to the crystals you see under the hand lens in Activity 9.

12. Make up a language experience story about ants. You may have experienced ants at a picnic, in cupboards, in a sugar bowl—or maybe you've seen red ants.

13. Create a newspaper published by the ant colony which reports on the trouble the "two bad ants" had in the world of humans.

14. Pretend you are an ant for several days. Each day write about your experiences in a journal; do this individually or as a whole class.

15. Do an "ant interview." One child dresses in an ant costume while the reporter interviews him or her. Questions and answers made up ahead by groups of children could serve as closure for the unit.

16. Read nonfiction trade books on ants and other insects. Children may want to give short talks about additional information they have gained.

17. Learn some songs about ants from the music teacher. Are the lyrics correct ideas about ants or just silly?

18. Ask the library media specialist to help students find out if ants work for or against our environment: are they disease-bearing, destructive, or able to inflict harm on humans?

19. Add and subtract numbers of ants for math; make up word problems involving ants.

20. What dangers do household appliances pose for humans? Make a safety list for small children for such items as toaster, microwave, electrical socket, etc.

21. Read the instruction papers given with new household appliances. Review the safety features and hints for safe operation.

22. Read the instructions on an ant trap without opening the outside covering. How should it be used? What are the dangers to people?

23. Write and act out a classroom drama about safe operation of appliances. Make costumes from boxes, sheets, etc.

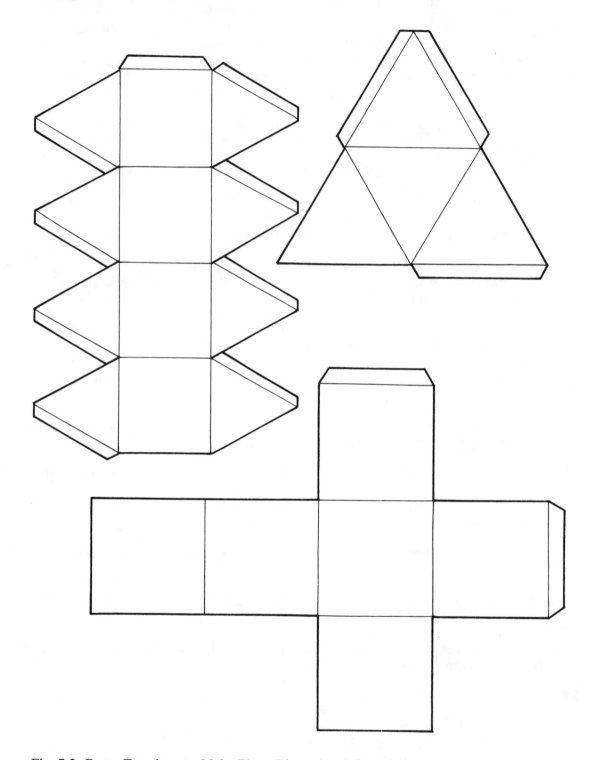

Fig. 7.2. Paper Templates to Make Three-Dimensional Crystal Shapes.

Related Books and References

Gackenbush, Dick. *Little Bug*. New York: Houghton Mifflin/Clarion Books, 1981.

Lobel, Arnold. *Grasshopper on the Road*. New York: Harper and Row, 1978.

Zim, Herbert, and Clarence Cottam. *Insects: A Guide to Familiar American Insects*. New York: Golden Press, 1951.

8

SPIDERS

The Very Busy Spider
Eric Carle
New York: Putnam, 1985

Summary

All day long, various animals attempt to keep the spider from completing her web. However, at day's end the exhausted spider has completed her task and woven a beautiful web.

Science Topic Areas

Daily activities of a spider, predatory behavior

Content Related Words

Web, predator, prey

Activities

1. Search for spider webs around the school. Use clean spray bottles filled with water as misters. Spray water on webs to make them easier to see and study. Dark places like corners of basements or unused areas are ideal locations to look for webs. You may need to use flashlights in these places. How does the spider react when a light is aimed at its web?

2. See how far a spider can spin a thread in one minute.

3. Spiders spin different sized threads, depending on the part of the web they are making. Ask a parent who sews to show samples of different kinds of thread and explain their purposes, e.g., carpet thread, quilting thread, monofilament nylon, polyester thread, cotton thread. Test the strength of the fibers by trying to break them.

4. Are spiders helpful or harmful to the environment? Do they provide good to people or are they destructive? Are there poisonous spiders? The library media center will have books on spiders that will explain the characteristics of the many varieties of these arachnids.

5. Keep a spider and web in a terrarium or large jar. Study the spider and write a class log about your observations. You will need to capture insects to feed the spider until its release.

6. Observe spiders with a hand lens to see how they react and move. They can also be seen on the overhead projector if they are first placed in a clear plastic tray which is set on the machine. Make a list of action or descriptive words to relate what you see, e.g., gliding, dropping, weaving.

7. Using yarn pom-poms and pipe cleaners, or modeling clay, make a model showing that spiders have two distinct body parts and eight legs (see figure 8.1).

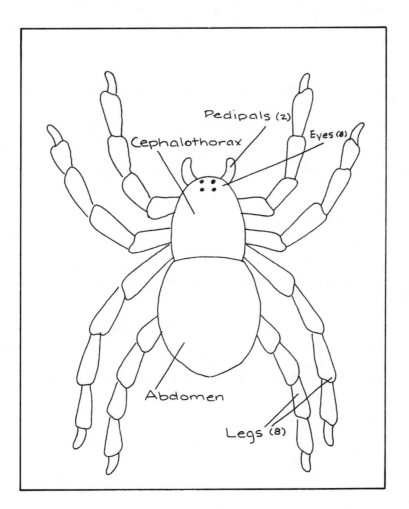

Fig. 8.1. Labeled Diagram of Common Spider.

8. Webs can also be made of pipe cleaners wound together. Paint them with thin school glue and sprinkle with glitter for holiday ornaments.

9. Use string art to make webs. Nails can be driven into a fiberboard base as a framework. String is wound from one nail to the next, wrapped around once, and taken to the next nail. This continues until the pattern of the entire web is completed. A large web made on a bulletin board can be used for the children's spider models. (See figure 8.2.)

10. Select words you have chosen to describe the spider and put them on small strips of paper. Attach these to the various lines of your web to make a "word web."

11. Edit a newspaper for spiders. Report on events of the spider community. There might be an advice column on the best shapes for webs or a gourmet cooking section on tasty insects the spider would enjoy. Remember, the spider itself is not an insect.

12. Conduct a "spider interview." Have one child dress up like a spider while reporters interview him or her. The costume should reflect the physical characteristics of the spider and serve as a source of questions. Questions can be made up ahead by groups of children.

13. Use *The Very Busy Spider* as a source of choral reading. A drum or other percussive accompaniment can emphasize the rhythmic language of the book.

14. Read other books by Eric Carle, such as *The Very Hungry Caterpillar*. How is the caterpillar's day like that of the spider? How is it different?

15. Read poems about spiders. Write some as a class or do individual couplets—two lines that are rhyming stanzas.

> Look at the spider
> It has a bug inside her

16. *Charlotte's Web* by E. B. White is a classic of children's literature. The teacher can read a chapter or two each day to the class as they study spiders, and finish the unit with a video or film of the story.

17. Does anyone know any songs about spiders? Can the school music specialist find some examples? Do these songs present biologically correct facts or are they just silly songs?

18. Is there a spider plant in the room? Why is it called that? What are the "baby spiders," and what is their purpose?

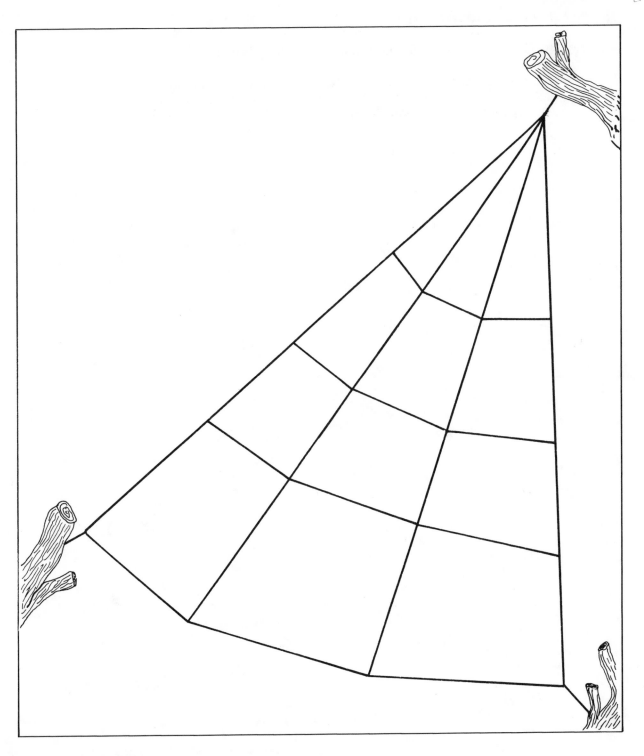

Fig. 8.2. A Spider Web Pattern.

Related Books and References

McDermott, Gerald. *Anasi the Spider*. New York: Holt, Rinehart and Winston, 1975.

McNulty, Faith. *The Lady and the Spider*. New York: Harper and Row, 1986.

White, E. B. *Charlotte's Webb*. New York: Harper and Row, 1952.

9

LADYBUGS

The Grouchy Ladybug
Eric Carle
New York: Thomas Crowell, 1977

Summary

The "grouchy" ladybug refuses to share the aphids on the leaves with the other ladybugs. Instead, she spends her day antagonizing other animals, all of which have their own particular protective adaptations to defend themselves. At the end of a very humbling and tiring day, a much wiser ladybug returns home, willing to share with others.

Science Topic Area

Protective adaptation, food chain, time, rotation of the earth, animal characteristics, sequencing

Content Related Words

Aphid, ladybug (ladybird), adaptation

Activities

1. Before finishing the book (after the whale page) have children predict the ending. Write some alternative endings.

2. Study the pictures of a ladybug. Use felt or paper pieces to construct a large ladybug on a flannel board. (Use the example shown in figure 9.1.) Label body parts and functions. Be sure to get the proper number of legs, wings, body parts. The number of spots will vary with different species. Make a similar cutout of an aphid. How are the insects alike and different?

3. Make thumbprint ladybugs or "pet rock" ladybugs.

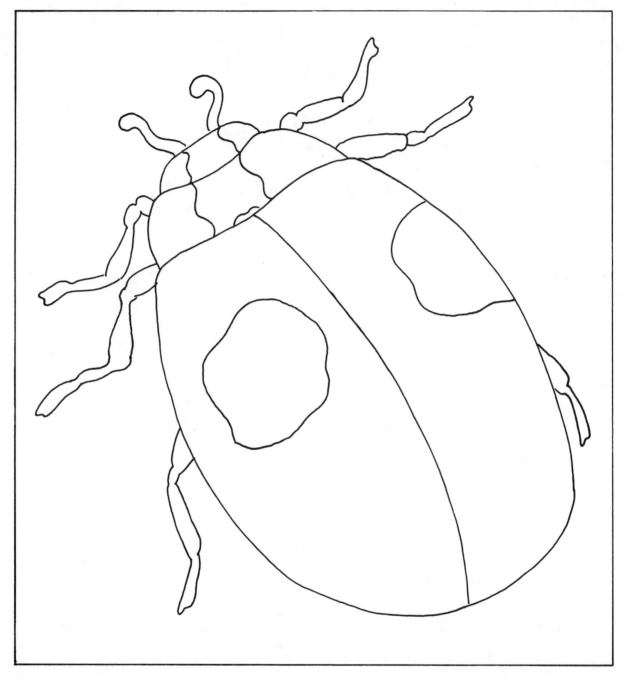

Fig. 9.1. A Ladybug Outline for Craft Activities.

4.   Using clear plastic boxes, make "bug houses" (see fig. 9.2) to hold insects you get by sweep-netting a field or lawn. Study these insects in class, then release them. (See activity 1 of *The Tiny Seed*.)

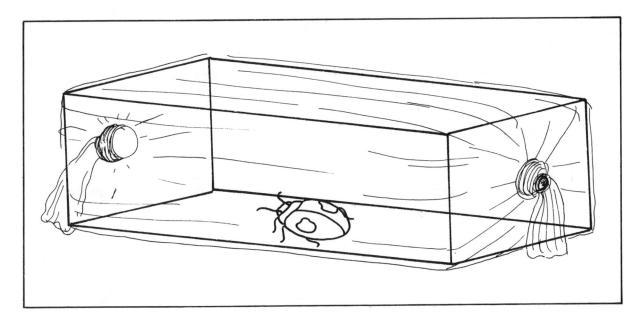

Fig. 9.2. "Bughouse" for Observing Insects.

5.   Chart the animals in the book, using these categories:

   (a)   classification of animal (mammal, insect, etc.)

   (b)   natural habitat

   (c)   size of animal

   (d)   type of food eaten

   (e)   use to mankind

   Children can make individual cards for each animal with this information on them.

6.   Select two characteristics for each animal in the book. Write each one on a separate card until you have twenty-four cards—two for each animal. Give each child one card. Everyone then walks around the room comparing cards and looking for someone who has a card bearing another characteristic of their animal. The name of the animal is not listed on the card. Students must find two cards that describe the same animal and decide which animal it is. If the group is larger, more cards can be made for each animal:

three characteristics for each of twelve animals, or thirty-six cards in total. The statements provided below are intended as examples of descriptions of some of the twelve animals in the book.

Yellow Jacket

Despite my average length of one inch, my protective defense can cause great discomfort, or even death, to humans. I do not have two or four legs and am very essential to the reproduction of many species of the plant kingdom.

Boa Constrictor

There are forty to sixty species of this animal, which are found mainly in warm regions. They depend on neither legs nor feet for locomotion. The young are born alive, not from eggs, and can grow to a length of 25 feet.

Skunk

I am a member of the weasel family and prefer to eat rodents, rats and birds, although I will eat plant material. For defense I emit a foul odor that can reach up to twenty feet.

Lobster

My flipper tail helps me navigate as I scavenge dead matter. I also feed on seaweed and live animals. My visibility is good because my eyes are located at the end of movable stalks.

Note: A children's encyclopedia will provide excellent ideas for animal descriptions.

7. List the different words the author uses for "meet." Look in a thesaurus for more words that mean "encounter."

8. Practice the proper form of introducing people. Write out these introductions to show use of quotation marks.

9. Write poems about the grouchy ladybug and the nice ladybug. Use contrasting adjectives and figurative language such as similes.

10. Write a paragraph explaining why you think the ladybug changed her attitude.

11. The ladybug is also known as a ladybird beetle. What famous nursery rhyme does this bring to mind? Can you change the words of that tale and fit in some adventures of this ladybug? Try to keep the same rhythm.

12. How many hours does the book cover? Is that a whole day? Which hours are A.M. and which are P.M.? Set up a sundial on the playground and mark the shadow length to correspond to the clock faces in the book. (See activity 6 of *Shadows*.)

13. Make your own personal time line showing where you are or what you are doing at each time shown on the clocks in the book. Does this time line cover your entire day? Do one for a school day and one for a vacation day.

14. Work with simple fractions—half hour, quarter hour, etc. This concept might be explained in terms of class length, recess time, the duration of a TV program, etc.

15. Select an animal from the book and pantomime how it protects itself.

16. Animals sometimes protect themselves through the use of camouflage. Design a yet-undiscovered animal with very special adaptations for survival. These can be drawn or painted, or created from odd bits of cloth, wood, colored paper, and packing materials, which are glued to a stiff sheet of paper. Give purposes for the animal's adaptation and see if children can guess which one it is. Invent a "grouchy animal" that

    (a)   rips its food apart before swallowing it

    (b)   squeezes its enemies to death

    (c)   can hide anywhere without being seen

    (d)   lives in the cracks of walks

    (e)   has skin "harder than nails"

    (f)   poisons its enemies in a blink of its eye

    (g)   uses beauty to lure its enemies

    (h)   can change the size of its mouth to fit its prey

17. To show comparative size, find other objects that are about the same size as each animal in the book. For the larger animals, make outlines on the playground to show size. On a smaller scale, make a mobile of the various animals using drawings or silhouettes or origami (see figure 9.3).

18. Listen to recordings about animals, e.g., Rimsky-Korsakov's "Flight of the Bumblebee." Do some creative movements to these selections. Try to imitate the sounds and movements of other animals in the book.

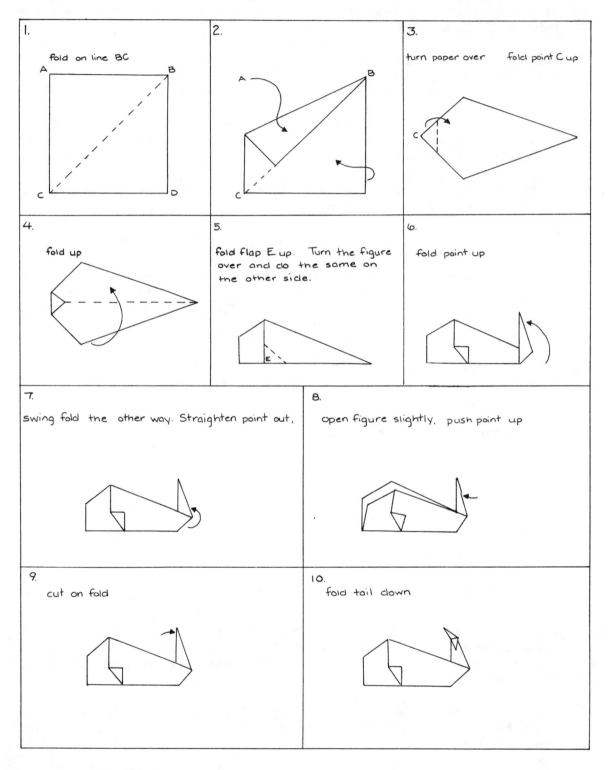

Fig. 9.3. An Origami Whale.

19. Are there songs in your school music book or a library song book about any of these animals?

20. On a world map, locate and mark the natural habitats of the animals the ladybug visited. Was a journey like this possible in a day?

21. Name some wild animals native to your country. How do they protect themselves? Does the government protect them?

22. Ask the library media specialist to obtain films or videos on topics such as the balance of nature, endangered species of animals, or wildlife refuge centers.

Related Books and References

Gackenbush, Dick. *Little Bug*. New York: Houghton Mifflin/Clarion Books, 1981.

Rimsky-Korsakov, Nikolai. "Flight of the Bumblebee." (E.g., The Boston Pops Orchestra, Arthur Fiedler conducting. RCA Victor recording.)

Saint-Saens, Camille. *Carnival of the Animals*. (E.g., The New York Philharmonic, Leonard Bernstein conducting. Columbia recording.)

Zim, Herbert, and Clarence Cottam. *Insects: A Guide to Familiar American Insects*. New York: Golden Press, 1951.

10

FISH

Swimmy

Leo Lionni
New York: Pantheon Books (Random House), 1963

Summary

A tuna swallows an entire school of fish, except for Swimmy. Sad and lonely, the little black fish explores the wonders of the ocean until he becomes part of a school of red fish. Here, in the middle of these fish, he feels safe.

Science Topic Areas

Schooling behavior of fish, predator-prey relationships, varieties of fish, ocean life

Content Related Words

Schooling (of fish), protection, behavior (biological meaning)

Activities

1. Before reading the story, discuss the saying "There is safety in numbers." Does the saying have an additional or different meaning after reading the story?

2. What are the characteristics that make a fish unique? Make a chart comparing fish and humans, e.g., fish breathe through gills but people breathe through their lungs.

3. Photographic stores have glass slide mounts. Place a few scales from a fish between the layers of glass and show them on a slide projector or examine them under a microscope. Each scale has a series of rings on it. Count the rings to determine the age of the fish. (See figure 10.1.)

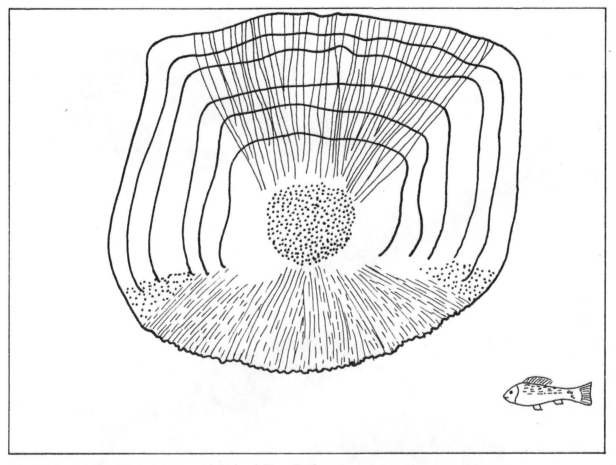

Fig. 10.1. A Magnified six-year-old Striped Bass Scale.

4. There is tremendous variety in the shape and size of fish. Why is this so? Make silhouettes of several unique fish (see figure 10.2) and put them on a wall display of an underwater environment. Colored tissue paper and watercolors make efficient and realistic backgrounds for ocean scenes.

5. Fish live at different depths in the ocean. This is called the water column. When placing the fish silhouettes on the display, follow these general rules:

    (a) Surface area—small fish, floating algae, and plankton

    (b) Middle depths—quick-moving fish, fish with streamlined body shapes, predatory fish

    (c) Bottom/floor area—slow-moving fish, fish which hide in or blend with the ocean bottom, flat fish, sea creatures which eat food that collects on the ocean floor

6. Identify the sea creatures in the story that are not fish. Look up some important characteristics that make each of those animals unique. Include the means of protection it uses.

Fig. 10.2. Representative Silhouettes of Salt Water Fish.

7. Make a set of "Sea Creature Rummy" cards based on the animals and plants in the book. Have four cards for each creature. When it is time to lay down groups of four similar cards, the student must also give a fact about the animal or plant. Pictures can be from nature or sporting magazines, or hand-sketched. You could use commercially made cards to play "Go Fish" and learn some facts about the fish they portray.

8. Dramatize the story of Swimmy. Include additional details on Swimmy's enemies, how fish protect themselves, why they travel in "schools," where they live, what they eat. The terms "predator-prey relationship" and "protective adaptation" can be used here.

9. Watch a video about life in the ocean, especially regarding the world of fish, and then critique the film. Leave the assignment open-ended without a particular set criteria and see how many different ways the children relate to the same experience.

10. If there is an aquarium in your area, the teacher might arrange a field trip to visit it. Sometimes a staff member will come to class before the visit to discuss what the children will see.

11. A classroom aquarium can be set up and maintained. A pet store can supply an equipment list and advise you on the choice and care of fish. Have the children help with all stages of setting up the aquarium and getting the water ready. Try to have the fish delivered while students are in class.

12. Make a class book about the aquarium. Ask each child to contribute a story and an illustration about setting up or maintaining the aquarium. You might duplicate these so that everyone has a personal copy to keep.

13. Fish are part of the food chain. Small fish are eaten by bigger fish which are eaten by even bigger fish, etc. Some are eaten by people. Discuss the food chain and the various means by which people can catch fish, e.g., fishing poles, nets, spears, etc. Is deep-sea fishing like fresh water fishing?

14. States usually publish a handbook of rules and regulations for citizens of that state. Get a copy from the library media center and check the regulations governing fishing near your home, e.g., need for a license, time of year it is permitted, etc.

15. Visit a fish market or grocery store and see how many different sea animals can be purchased in your area. Where do the various creatures originate, e.g., Alaskan king crab, Maine lobster. What are the prices per pound? If the entire class cannot go, a list of questions might be written for a small group visit, a telephone interview, or a guest appearance, e.g., Where do you buy the seafood? How long does it stay fresh in the store?

16. Some restaurants that specialize in seafood conduct school tours, followed by a sample of their products.

17. What are the advantages of fish and ocean animals as a food group for human beings? What do industries do with the remains of these animals after they have been processed for market?

18. Using the *World Almanac*, identify the countries that engage in commercial fishing. List the top ten in order. Where is the United States ranked?

19. We speak of a "school of fish." Other animals are referred to by unique names, e.g., a den of lions, a flock of geese (or a gaggle if they're not in flight), etc. How many of these do you know? Ask at home for ideas.

20. Swimmy was accepted and liked because his color was different from that of the other fish. Does this hold true in human society when one person is different because of color, religion, background, or physical impairment? What should our attitude be? What is it in reality? Write a description of a day at school from the viewpoint of a new student who is "different" in some way and compare it with a description from the viewpoint of one of the "regular kids" who is in the class.

21. What method of illustration is used in this story? Try to use this method to create a picture, placemat, bookmark, or book cover. Use clear adhesive film to seal and strengthen your piece.

22. Fish are often used in artwork. *Gyotaku* is the process of Japanese fish printing. Use a very flat fish which has been washed with soap and water and dried. Place the fish on several layers of newspaper and be sure the fins and tail are spread open. With a small brush, cover the fish with a water-based ink or acrylic paint, working against the grain of the scales, then smoothing them out. The print may be made on rice paper, a clean, plain T-shirt, a piece of cloth, etc. Press the item on the inked fish and rub firmly, but gently. Peel the paper or cloth off slowly to avoid smudging. (If a T-shirt is used, you may wish to put a layer or two of scrap material inside the shirt so the ink does not bleed through to the back.)

23. Make and fly Japanese fish kites (see figure 10.3).

24. Listen to the impressionist composition called *La Mer* by Claude Debussy. What images of the ocean does this create for you?

Related Books and References

Debussy, Claude. *La Mer*. (E.g., in the Columbia Twentieth Century Collection.)

Lionni, Leo. *Fish Is Fish*. New York: Alfred Knopf, 1987.

Zim, Herbert, and Hurst Shoemaker. *Fishes: A Guide to Familiar American Species*. New York: Golden Press, 1955.

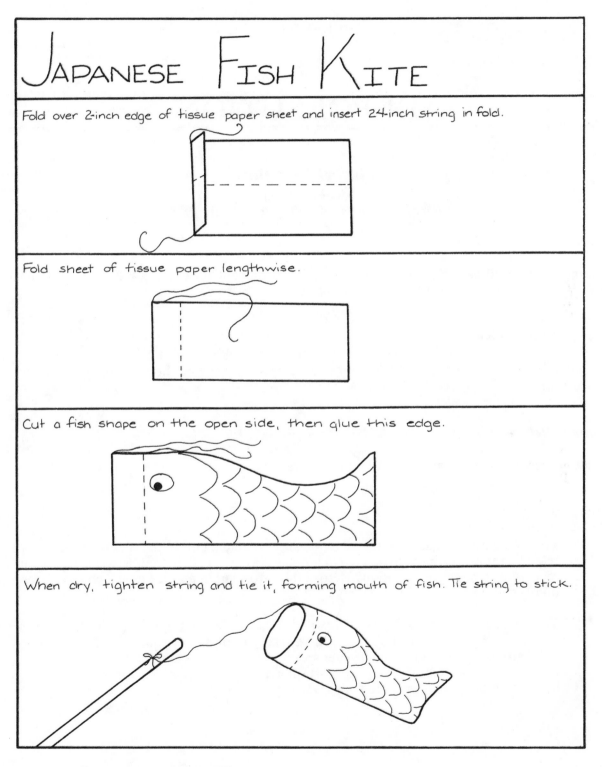

JAPANESE FISH KITE

Fold over 2-inch edge of tissue paper sheet and insert 24-inch string in fold.

Fold sheet of tissue paper lengthwise.

Cut a fish shape on the open side, then glue this edge.

When dry, tighten string and tie it, forming mouth of fish. Tie string to stick.

Fig. 10.3. Making a Japanese Fish Kite.

11

AIR POLLUTION

Michael Bird-Boy

Tomie dePaola
Englewood Cliffs, N.J.: Prentice-Hall, 1975

Summary

A large black cloud causes many changes in the environment of a young boy. When Michael locates the factory that is producing the pollution, he helps to solve the problem.

Science Topic Areas

Air pollution and its effects, pollution control, weather, seasons of the year, bees and honey, manufacturing

Content Related Words

Pollution, environment, assembly line, sequence, factory

Activities

1. What is pollution? Does your local newspaper contain a pollution index or other type of report on pollution in your area? Do you have a TV weather channel or newscast that reports the amount of pollution? Record this information and see how it changes over a number of days.

2. You are running for political office and believe air pollution must be lessened or eliminated. How many different arguments can you find to support your cause? Assign small groups of children to act as your speech writers to develop a short TV spot dealing with the various issues. Or stage a short interview with people who are greatly affected by air pollution, such as those with respiratory diseases.

3. If you could interview a bee, flower, or animal, what might they have to say about pollution? Write this story from their point of view.

4. Air pollution is only one form of pollution. What other kinds are a problem? Do these exist in your neighborhood or town? What about in your own home, its problems, and what is being done? Acid rain is a good example which is often in newspapers and magazines, and on TV.

5. Young people can fight solid waste pollution by participating in litter cleanup programs and gathering empty bottles for recycling or refunds. Be a part of a project of this type.

6. What can adults do to help lessen pollution? What can politicians or factory owners do? How could you let your views about pollution be known by persons in power? Carry out some of your ideas.

7. The book shows how plants and animals are affected by air pollution. How are objects affected?

   (a) Divide the class into groups and assign them to various outside sections of the school building. Do they see dirt and discoloration or other signs of pollution? Mark the areas with colored stickers, then have the class as a whole examine the various sites and discuss the problem.

   (b) Others might visit an old cemetery to see which tombstones have been affected by pollution and weathering. List the death dates that appear on the ones most severely affected.

   (c) Hang a white cloth out the school window. Examine it after a few days and see how it has changed. (Rain can ruin the effect so try to do this on dry days.)

   (d) Melt snow, then pour it through filter paper or a clean cloth. What do you see?

   (e) Help someone wash a car. What does it look like after sitting outside for a day or so?

8. Michael Bird-Boy loved nature and did not want it ruined by pollution. Select one thing you love about nature that could be adversely affected by pollution and write about it. Tell why you like it and how pollution could hurt it. Perhaps this is something that has already happened, e.g., toxic chemicals in your favorite fishing stream.

9. If possible, invite a beekeeper in to explain about raising bees, kinds of bees, the jobs they have within the bee colony, types of hives, use of beeswax and honeycombs, etc. Or have small groups of students research these topics in the library media center and present them to the class.

10. Check a local gourmet or specialty shop to find out how many different kinds of honey are sold in your town. Also list the price and size of the container. Are some types more expensive? Where is the honey packaged? Are they all natural products or are some artificially flavored?

11.   Use honey in a baking project:

Michael's Honey Cake

1 cup quick-cooking oats
1½ cups flour
pinch of salt
1 teaspoon ginger
½ cup shortening
1 cup boiling water
1 teaspoon soda
1 teaspoon cinnamon
¼ teaspoon cloves
¾ cup sugar
2 eggs

Pour boiling water over oats; let stand covered for 20 minutes. Cream shortening and sugar; beat in honey. Stir in eggs and oatmeal. Sift in all dry ingredients and mix well. Bake at 350 degrees for 60 to 65 minutes in a well-greased and floured 13"x9"x2" pan. Leave in pan and frost.

Boss Lady's Honey Frosting

¼ cup butter or margarine (softened)
⅓ cup honey
½ cup flaked coconut
¼ cup chopped pecans or walnuts

Cream honey and butter until light and fluffy. Stir in coconut and nuts. Frost cooled cake. Have a celebration!

12.   Bee stings can cause allergic reactions or even death for some humans. Find out what you would do for a classmate who had this allergy if they were stung at school. Ask parents or other adults what home remedies they use for bee stings (assuming no allergy is involved); e.g., some people make a paste of meat tenderizer and water.

13.   Some bees can be very harmful. Watch for news items or magazine articles about killer bees.

14.   Gather various kinds of flowers or look at cross-sectional diagrams of flowers (see figure 11.) Where is the nectar located? Can you reach it without destroying the flower? How does the bee get to it?

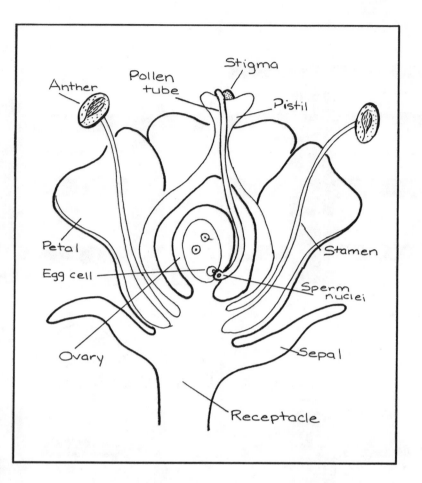

Fig. 11.1. Cross Section of a Flower.

15. The factory is efficient because it is automated. Set up an assembly line to make pipe cleaner bees. Each child or team will have one task to perform before passing the item on for the next step. You will need yellow and black 12-inch pipe cleaners, rulers, scissors, and small boxes for packing. (Each bee requires one yellow and two black pipe cleaners. See figure 11.2.) You might organize the work into the following roles:

   a. The Boss—starts, regulates, and stops work rate, e.g., if a breakdown occurs in the assembly line.

   b. Unpackers—give out black and yellow pipe cleaners.

   c. Cutters—cut half of the black pipe cleaners into five equal pieces, cut the others into two equal pieces.

   d. Cutters—cut yellow cleaners into two sections (4-inch and 8-inch).

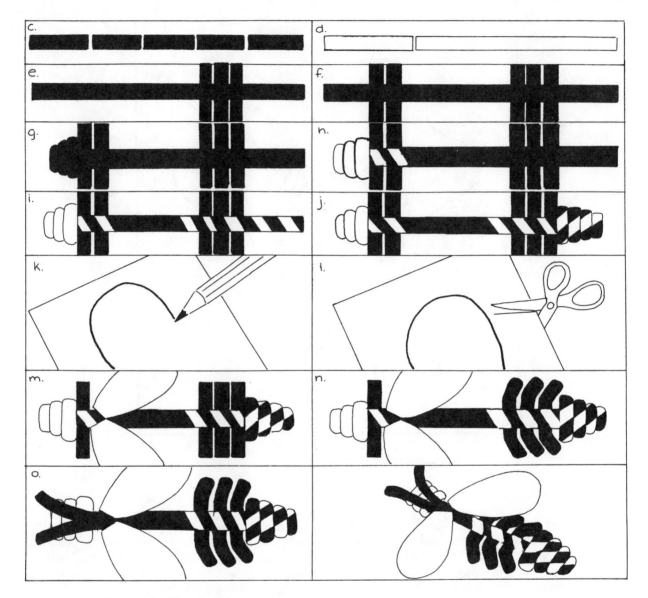

Fig. 11.2. An Assembly Line Activity.

e. Loopers—tie three short pieces of black pipe cleaner to half of a black pipe cleaner, 4 inches from one end.

f. Loopers—tie two pieces of black pipe cleaner to whole pipe cleaner (2 inches from other end to form wing and antennae ends.

g. Headers—twist front end of long black pipe cleaner into a head.

h.   Wrappers—wrap the 4-inch yellow piece around the head.

i.   Twisters—twist the 8-inch yellow piece around the tail and leg sections.

j.   Coilers—coil the tail end to form the abdomen.

k.   Tracers—trace wings onto transparent sheet.

l.   Wing Cutters—cut wing sections out of transparent sheet.

m.   Gluers—glue wings onto wing holders.

n.   Leggers—bend legs into shape.

o.   Shapers—bend antennae into shape.

p.   Inspector—checks completed bees for quality.

q.   Disassemblers—take apart defective bees for remanufacture.

r.   Packers—pack completed bees for "shipping" or "storage."

16. Bees and honey are mentioned in many common sayings such as "busy as a bee" and "sweeter than honey." Ask others to share sayings they know and add these to any displays you have made.

17. Music has been written about bees, e.g., "The Flight of the Bumblebee" by Nikolai Rimsky-Korsakov. What picture does the composer want you to visualize? How does he achieve this?

Related Books and References

Dickson, Naida. "Killer Bees: How Serious a Threat?" *Current Science* (November 1, 1985).

Peet, Bill. *The Wump World*. Boston: Houghton Mifflin, 1970.

Rimsky-Korsakov, Nikolai. "The Flight of the Bumblebee." (E.g., The Boston Pops Orchestra, Arthur Fiedler conducting. RCA Victor recording.)

12

ADAPTATIONS OF ANIMALS

Chipmunk Song
Joanne Ryder
New York: E. P. Dutton, 1987

Summary

This story portrays the life of a chipmunk as it deals with the challenges of the changing seasons. These include: food gathering, ways to keep warm or cool, and means of avoiding predators. The reader's imagination is heightened by illustrations which show a boy simulating the chipmunk's activities.

Science Topic Areas

Animal adaptations, protective behavior, communication, seasons, annual life cycle of the chipmunk, food gathering for winter survival

Content Related Words

Camouflage, hibernation, predator, prey, insulation

Activities

1. Chipmunks are able to hide from predators because of their protective coloration and patterned belt. Invent "imaginary critters" from around the classroom or school yard and have a scavenger hunt. Which are hard or easy to find? Write descriptions of the "critters" and the environment in which they can hide best.

2. In nature, larger animals often eat smaller animals, which in turn eat even smaller animals. Locate all the animals pictured in the book (some are hiding very well) and decide which ones would eat others. Which eat only plants? What different plant food sources do you see?

(Teachers should be sure the children have located ferns, grasses, flowers, nectar, blackberries, acorns, red berries, roots, thistle seeds, turtle, starling, evening grosbeak, blackbird, butterfly, deer, mole, weasel, toad, mouse, hawk, chipmunk, worm, and grub.)

3. After you have listed all the plants and animals in the book, have children hold a large card or make a paper bag mask representing each item on the list. To see how the food chain works, place the children in a semicircle. Ask each represented animal what plant or animal it would eat. Attach a string or length of yarn between "animal" and the food source. (See figure 12.1.) When everyone has had a turn, discuss the interrelationships of the plants and animals. After the discussion, cut one of the strings. What effect will it have on the balance of nature? Cut another string. How long before there is no food for any animal?

4. Self-protection is a major concern of animals. What dangers does the chipmunk face? How does he avoid them? Have children discuss the dangers they might encounter at home, school, or play, and how these can be avoided. Make safety poster to illustrate these ideas.

5. Using string or yarn, mark off an area 1 square yard in size. Scatter colored toothpicks in the area. Give a student a specific number of seconds to pick up individual toothpicks.

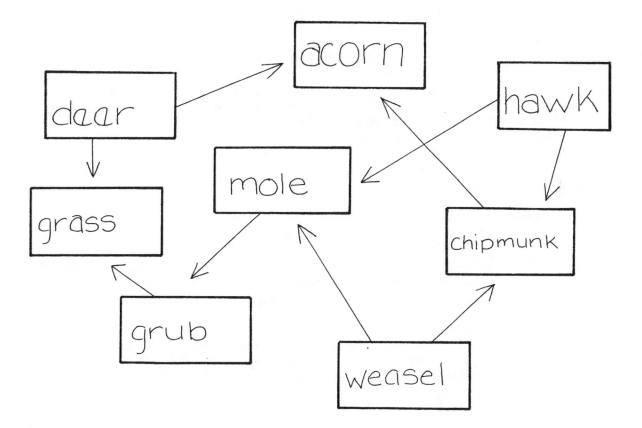

Fig. 12.1. A Forest Food Chain.

How many of each color are chosen? What can you conclude about the color of the toothpicks and the background? Continue for a second timed try. What are the results? What color is the easiest to see? Which is the most difficult to see?

6. Visit a site where you can dig a shallow hole or where an existing hole in the ground exposes soil vertically. Make sketches or take samples of each soil layer to form a profile. If the soil is dry, a profile can be collected in one piece by applying a sheet of clear adhesive paper to the side of the soil cut. Compare the kinds of soil and the objects found in each layer.

7. This book shows many wildflowers and plants. Gather examples from your area and observe the flower, leaves, and stems. A local garden club or extension service agent may be able to provide you with an area identification guide or use a general field guide to wildflowers to name the specimens and their parts.

8. Have an outdoor "animal food hunt." List the foods you find, e.g., acorns, berries, etc. Where are these foods found? Do you live in an area where forest animals come into yards and gardens? What types of food do they eat, e.g., lettuce from gardens, seed from bird feeders?

9. Bring in different types of nuts. Identify and categorize both the shells and the nuts. Be able to match the shell and the nutmeat and describe them, e.g., almond shells are smooth, porous, and easily broken, but the rust-colored nut has tiny ridges on it. If possible, also bring in the covering that encases the nut and see how it acts as a protective device. Cut the nuts in half and examine the inside. Observe the texture, coloring, etc. Rub the nut on blotter paper. Why does it leave a spot?

10. If you can gather enough acorns, give a few to each student. What coloration change is there between acorns? Can the nut be opened without implements? Which ones are easier to peel? What is the inside part like? What can you conclude about the chipmunk from these observations?

11. Keep a chameleon in a large class terrarium. Observe how it changes color against various backgrounds.

12. People can "change color" or camouflage themselves. What clothing would best help people go unnoticed? When or where would this most likely be used?

13. Investigate the concept of "reverse camouflage." Make or color objects so they are easy to find. Hang them on various backgrounds to judge their effectiveness. Bring in hats or apparel that exemplify this, e.g., hunters' or joggers' clothing. Or make costumes to show this.

14. The chipmunk's heart beats faster as it flees its predators. A child's heartbeat increases with activity. Check pulse rates after walking and running. Record these scores and use them to calculate averages or make graphs.

15. To observe the pulse, push a flat-headed thumbtack into the bottom of a wooden kitchen match and place it on the child's wrist, over the pulse beat. Be sure the arm is resting on a table. (See figure 12.2.) The match will vibrate as the heart beats.

16. Identify places on the earth where people have adapted to having little sunlight during midwinter. Write about living in semidarkness all winter. What would life be like for these people? How would your life change if you moved there?

17. The chipmunk lives underground to keep cool or warm, depending on the season. How do people control the temperature of their rooms? How does the temperature of our rooms change from floor to ceiling or from inside wall to outside wall? Thermistor strips simplify temperature measurement.

18. How do people prepare their houses, lawns, gardens, cars, and themselves for the winter, e.g., by bringing in lawn furniture, and checking storm windows. Ask parents and grandparents what this involved when they were younger. Are the answers different? Was there more home food preservation, a need to install snow tires, etc.?

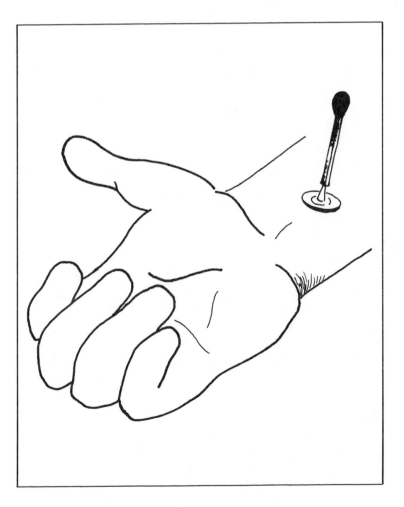

Fig. 12.2. Observing Your Pulse.

19. The chipmunk could store things in the cool earth, as did the early settlers of our country. What other ways did people use to preserve food before the canning process and refrigeration were common? Do we preserve any foods this way, e.g., fruits, beef?

20. "The Chipmunk's Song" by Randall Jarrell also tells of the chipmunk's winter preparation. How is his account similar to Ryder's? How is the environment of the chipmunk different in the two works?

Related Books and References

Jarrell, Randall. "The Chipmunk." In *Piping Down the Valleys Wild: Poetry for the Young of All Ages*, edited by Nancy Larrick. New York: Delacorte Press, 1985.

McCloskey, Robert. *Blueberries for Sal*. New York: Viking Press, 1948.

Ryder, Joanna. *Simon Underground*. New York: Harper and Row, 1976.

13

NUTRITION

Gregory, the Terrible Eater
Mitchell Sharmat
New York: Scholastic, 1980

Summary

Goats are supposed to eat junk, but Gregory wanted only food that was good for him, like vegetables and eggs. His parents worried because he had no taste for boxes and cans, but a compromise eventually resulted in a balanced diet for everyone concerned.

Science Topic Areas

Nutrition, balanced diet, food requirements

Content Related Words

Nutrition, calories, protein, carbohydrates, fats, vitamins, and minerals

Activities

1. Junk food can have different meanings for different people. How does this concept differ for you and your parents, and Gregory and his parents?

2. If you were a nutrition expert, what criteria would you use to determine if food is "junk," e.g., the quantity of fat, protein, calories, vitamins, etc., it contains.

3. Select several food items that the class agrees are "junk food" and several that are considered "good for you." Compare the items by looking at the nutritional information on the packaging.

4. Keep a journal of the snack foods you eat during a week. Are they really junk foods? What snacks would be nutritional?

5. Take a survey of class favorites: favorite fruit, vegetable, main course, dessert, after school snack, etc. Make a bar graph of two or three winners in each category. Compare this to a few of the class's least favorites. Try the same survey with a group of adults, such as parents and teachers. Do you find more similarities or differences? Who eats more "junk food"?

6. Check labels on common items like baby food, peanut butter, fruit punch, cereal, canned vegetables and fruits, and bread to learn what additives have been included during processing. Do these enhance nutritional value? Help preserve the item? Make it look more attractive?

7. A vitamin pill bottle lists several vitamins and minerals that people need in their diets. Assign one of these to each student. Why is this vitamin or mineral necessary? In what foods is it found? Record the information on a large chart.

8. Have a cafeteria person talk to the class on how the food service staff plans meals to be nutritious and yet appeal to students? Which meals are the most popular?

9. What are the four major food groups? What are your favorite items in each group? Which are your least favorite?

10. Analyze the menu from your school cafeteria for a week and see if each meal contains food from each group.

11. Make a collage of pictures with the theme "I Am What I Eat." Include your favorite foods and items that reflect your personality.

12. Using the foods that you and your classmates most favored, plan a well-balanced meal representing the four food groups (milk and dairy; bread and cereal; protein foods such as fish, eggs, peanuts, and soybeans; and fruits and vegetables). How many calories does this meal contain? Is it appropriate for the number of calories you require? The following chart, which shows examples of what a healthy child needs each day, will help in all your meal-planning activities.

Daily Needs for Children (Ages 4 to 10)

Milk—four servings a day

  Milk: ¾ to 1 cup

  Cheese: ¾ to 1½ ounces

  Yogurt: ¾ to 1 cup

Meat—2 or more servings a day

  Meat, fish, poultry: 2 to 3 ounces

Eggs: 1 whole

Peanut butter: 2 to 3 tablespoons

Luncheon meat: 2 slices

Vegetables, fruits—4 or more servings a day

Orange or tomato juice: ½ to 1 cup

Strawberries: 1 cup

Spinach, broccoli, carrots: ¼ cup

Cantaloupe: ¼ to ½

Potato: ½ to 1

Apple, banana: ½ to 1

Breads and cereals: 4 or more servings a day

Bread: 1 to 2 slices

Dry cereal (unsweetened): 1 cup

Cooked cereal, rice, pasta: ½ cup

13. Use the chart below to answer the questions that follow the chart. Make up some similar questions for one another to answer.

Approximate Daily Protein and Calorie Needs, by Age
(Source: RDA—National Academy of Sciences, 1979)

Age	Protein (grams)		Calories	
7-10	34	34	2400	2400
11-14	46	45	2200	2700
15-18	46	56	2100	2800
19-22	44	56	2100	2900
23-50	44	56	2000	2700
51-70	44	56	1800	2400

(a) How many calories a day should you eat according to the chart?

(b) Do you need more or fewer calories than your mother? father?

(c) At what age will you need the most calories? the fewest?

(d) In general, do men or women need more calories?

(e) How much protein do you need now? At what age do females need more protein than males?

(f) After you reach adulthood, does your need for protein change?

(g) Will your need for protein increase or decrease as you grow older?

14. This chart does not take into account some very important facts about people. Can you name some, e.g., height and weight differences?

15. Breakfast is supposed to be the most important meal of the day. Compare calories and nutritional value of several breakfasts: cereal and milk, bacon-eggs-toast, juice and coffee, or a pastry and milk. Include different types of cold cereals (presweetened, sugarless, containing dried fruit) and various hot cereals.

16. Survey ten people of different ages to see what they eat for breakfast. Who eats the most nutritious breakfast, from what you learned above?

17. Make a simple cookie recipe following the standard directions. Make another batch using three-fourths the normal amount of sugar, and a third batch using one-half the sugar. Is there a taste difference? What can you infer from this?

18. Grind peanuts in a blender to make peanut butter. Compare the taste to a commercial peanut butter. What ingredients are added to the processed item? Why is this done? Is it necessary?

20. Adults sometimes use various devices to get children to eat. Write or tell about how someone disguised food or played a game to get you to eat. Perhaps the food was arranged in a particular way to make it fun to eat, e.g., pancakes with Mickey Mouse ears and chocolate chips for a face.

21. Invent a food arrangement, such as a salad, that resembles a particular object. Write a recipe including a list of ingredients and the way they are to be cut and arranged.

22. Some of us no longer like a food we once loved. Write a story that explains what happened, e.g., "Too Many Green Peppers Can Make You Green." Sometimes we learn to like a food we once disliked. Invent slogans for these, e.g., Don't Squash Squash, Spinach is Special.

23. Proper exercise is needed along with proper eating. Have the physical education teacher show you some exercises that are good to help you stay in shape. What are some that would help young people who might have a weight problem? Should there be any limits on how much food young people eat?

24. How many different books can you find in your local bookstore on diets? How many diet aids are available in the local drug store? What promises do they make? Are these products safe?

25. Discuss anorexia and bulimia—the differences, why they occur, what the results can be. If possible, interview someone who has overcome an eating disorder or have the school nurse give you details on it.

26. Compare magazines that are aimed at specific groups of people, e.g., *Sports Illustrated, Modern Maturity, Good Housekeeping, Young Miss*. Which ones contain advertisements for food products? Do these ads emphasize good nutrition or try to sell "junk" food? Bring in examples of the ads and see how they differ.

27. Write and perform a TV commercial for a new super-nutritional food. What is the food and what does your company claim it will do for people? How will this be beneficial to them? How do you convince people they need to buy your product?

28. It is the twenty-first century. A pill has been invented which contains all the nutrients needed by people. Eating, as we know it, will become obsolete since it will be possible to take a pill instead. Write or discuss your reactions to this. Do you think taking a food pill is preferable or are there reasons for wishing to retain the concept of food that must be prepared and then eaten?

29. For Christmas, or some other holiday, make a class cookbook containing recipes from students' families (avoid duplicates). Be sure to add a couple of favorites from Gregory's family—it is said that "laughter helps the digestion."

30. "Food for Thought": Ask various people why they think Americans spend so much money on nutritious pet food and worry about what their animals eat, when they stuff themselves with non-nutritious "junk" food.

Related Books and References

Hoban, Russell, and Lillian Hoban. *Bread and Jam for Frances*. New York: Scholastic Book Services, 1964.

Smith, Robert. *Chocolate Fever*. New York: Dell, 1978.

14

SOUND AND HEARING

I Have a Sister, My Sister Is Deaf

Jeanne Whitehouse Peterson
New York: Harper and Row, 1984

Summary

A young girl expresses much love for her younger deaf sister by the way she describes her many capabilities, as well as her limitations. Family life, recreation, and school are particularly emphasized as we see how a deaf child learns to communicate in a world of hearing people.

Science Topic Areas

Sound, hearing, hearing loss, communication (with and by a deaf person), characteristic sounds

Content Related Words

Vibration, hearing-impaired

Activities

1. Objects must vibrate to produce sound. Observe and describe what happens when you do the following:

   - Strike a tuning fork and dip it in water.
   - Sprinkle cereal flakes on a drum, then tap the top.
   - Stretch a rubber band between your fingers and have someone pluck it; stretch the elastic farther and pluck again.
   - Put your hand on the top of a radio that is playing.

2. What materials conduct sound best? Visit the music room and try the different percussion instruments—woodblocks, plastic blocks, wooden xylophone, metal xylophone, glasses (empty), glasses filled with water (can be tuned to play a scale), plastic drum heads, leather or hide drum heads, metal triangle. The loudest, clearest tone indicates the best conductor.

3. Make a telephone. Use two empty tin or plastic cans. Remove one end of the can and punch a hole in the other end. Connect the cans with at least fifteen feet of string which has been threaded through the hole and knotted so that it cannot slip out. Experiment with how long the string can be and still conduct sound. Dictate something over your phone for a friend to copy—did they really hear everything you said? Will wire work instead of the string?

4. Observe 10 minutes of silence in class. What sounds do you hear? Which ones would probably be blocked out by the normal class activities? Were any of the sounds so loud they would have interrupted a regular class? Do the sounds of the students change during the 10 minutes?

5. Conduct a class in which no spoken words or sounds are used. Discuss afterwards how people felt, how much was accomplished, ways they could communicate. Don't write out directions or any items that would not normally be put on the board.

6. Have groups of students wear earplugs for a certain length of time during the day. Be sure everyone gets a chance, and talk or write about the emotions they felt. Was it the same during class? recess? lunch?

7. Soon after the earplug experience, make a list of the various ways students with hearing problems can be accommodated in the regular classroom.

8. All hearing problems are not the same. Does your school check your hearing? If so, which kinds of tests do they use? Are specialty tests such as the Seashore Tests of Musical Capacity given? Perhaps the person who administers the tests could explain what the various purposes are before testing.

9. Because she was deaf, there were many things that the sister could not do. However, there were some activities she was able to do well. Compare these to your own abilities.

10. What do you think would be the biggest problem if your hearing were seriously impaired, e.g., talking on the phone? Write why this would bother you the most and how you might overcome the problem.

11. Watch a complete TV program with the sound turned off. Write down what you think the story was. (Don't look in the TV guide for clues or watch a repeat of a show you've seen.) Compare your story with someone who watched and heard the same show. Reverse roles the next day.

12. Is there a collection of instructional cassette tapes or recordings in your library media center? Obtain a tape of sound effects and listen to them. Can you identify them?

13. Make a tape of your own sound effects or try to tell a story in sound, e.g., "Morning at My House," "The Track Meet," etc.

14. Would it change your enjoyment of a movie if there were no sound effects or music in the background? Which is more important? What different kinds of music are used in various situations?

15. Study a plastic model or diagram of the ear to see the many parts it contains. Trace how the sound travels from the outside environment to the brain. What can happen to impair or destroy the hearing of a person? How can you tell if a baby has a hearing problem?

16. Have someone demonstrate various kinds of hearing aids and how they work.

17. Sing, together as a class, the first line of a very familiar song. Then stop singing and try to hear it in your head until the teacher signals for you to sing again. Were you all in the same place? Did you start on the same note?

18. Think of sounds that are pleasurable. Make a collage of magazine photos to illustrate those sounds, e.g., the noise of a baseball game, happy babies, etc.

19. Check the yellow pages of the telephone directory to see what specialized services are offered for persons with hearing problems. Why might you need to contact these various groups?

20. Get a pamphlet from an audiology center or ear doctor on the proper care of the ears. Discuss this in class and make posters for a hall display to indicate proper ear care and safety.

21. If you had a serious hearing impairment, could you attend special classes in your town? Where is the nearest school for the deaf? Is it a boarding school? What subjects would you study?

22. Deaf or hearing-impaired persons can learn to "hear" by reading lips and to "speak" through signed language and actual speech. Figure 14.1 shows the signed movements for two very common phrases.

23. Play charades, using book titles, TV shows, famous sayings. Agree on specific clues before beginning. Using teams will add competition to the activity.

24. Listen to the last movement of Ludwig von Beethoven's Symphony No. 9 in D Minor (the *Choral* Symphony), which was written after the composer was totally deaf. How was he able to do this?

25. The teacher might read a book to the class about Helen Keller, who suffered from multiple physical impairments.

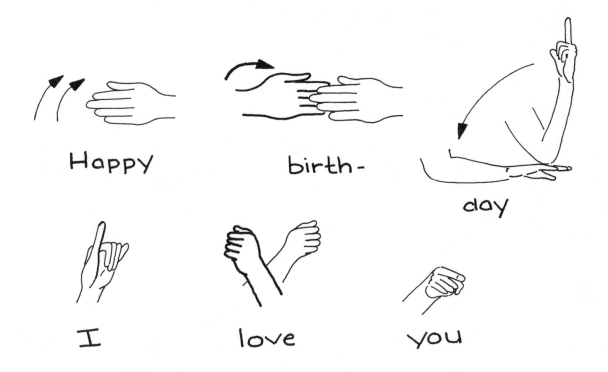

Fig. 14.1. Signed Language Movements.

Related Books and References

Beethoven, Ludwig von. *Symphony No. 9 in D Minor*. (E.g., the London Classical Players, Roger Norrington conducting. Angel recording.)

Bove, Linda. *Sesame Street Sign Language ABC*. New York: Random House/Children's Television Workshop, 1985.

Seldon, Bernice. *The Story of Annie Sullivan, Helen Keller's Teacher*. New York: Dell, 1987.

Part III
EARTH AND SPACE SCIENCE

15

TERRITORIAL AND ENVIRONMENTAL OWNERSHIP

It's Mine

Leo Lionni
New York: Alfred Knopf, 1986

Summary

Three frogs pass the time of day quibbling over who owns the earth, the air, and the water. A natural disaster makes them realize their foolishness and leads to an understanding of the situation.

Science Topic Areas

Ownership of the environment, defense of personal territory, and competition for space, air, water, food

Content Related Words

Ecology, environment, territory, cooperation, competition

Activities

1. Make segmented frogs (see cutout, figure 15.1) from construction paper and brass fasteners. Show how these animals move by manipulating the pieces.

2. Dramatize the story or attach sticks to the frogs you made and have a puppet show. Make a large mural of the pond environment to serve as your backdrop.

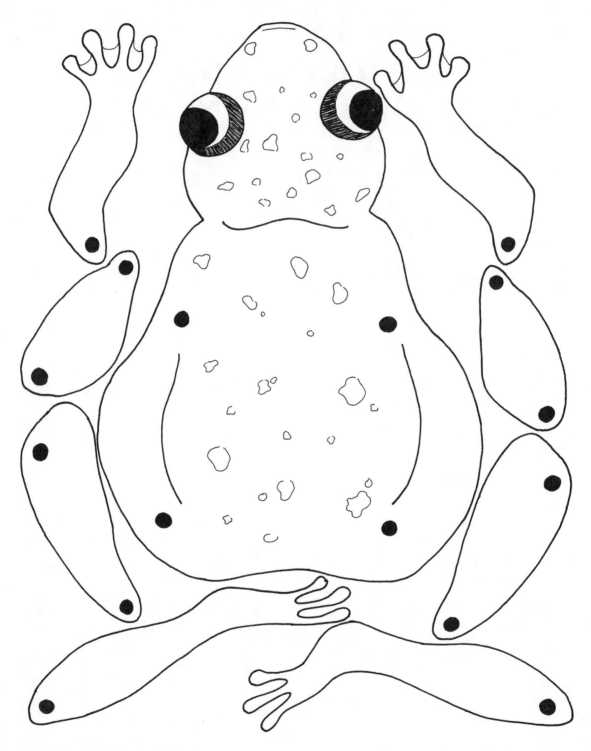

Fig. 15.1. The Segmented Frog.

3.   There are many kinds of beaches in the world—sandy, rocky, pebbly, swamps and mangroves, etc. Look in the library media center for travel magazine articles and photos that will help you learn more about these areas. For example, how are beaches used by people and animals, i.e., sandy beaches are good for human recreation, swamps provide breeding grounds for fish, etc.

4.   Create a wall collage of a beach scene. Make leaves by folding paper in half and cutting shapes, or cut them freehand. Compare the symmetry of these two methods. Which is more authentic looking? Do the same with rocks, flowers, butterflies, etc. Wallpaper samples and tissue boxes often have excellent designs to use.

5.   What events indicate that a storm is coming? Put them in proper sequence. What kinds of storms most often occur where you live? Write down the events of a day when the weather forecaster predicts a storm for your area. Are these similar to the events of the story?

6.   Have you ever been in a bad storm or flood? What were your feelings? Can you describe the destructive force of water?

7.   Divide the room into three groups of children and give each group one unique item to "control," e.g., the water fountain, the art supplies, the reading corner. Role play the characters in the book who refused to share. Discuss the problems that arise and how children feel about them.

8.   Write a sequel to the book. The frogs have learned to stop arguing and know they must share the environment. How do they spend their time now? What values do they have?

9.   Debate who "owns" outer space or the ocean floor. How is it decided who can build a space station, fish in the St. George's Banks, etc.? Have children represent various countries—the superpowers, developing nations, poor countries with large populations, small technologically advanced nations, etc.

10.   It is not possible to "buy" the air or the water, but people can buy land. Have the library media specialist save copies of the classified section of several newspapers to see what kind of land is available, e.g., house lots, farm acreage. Could you buy land next to a lake or ocean? Do you live in an area where you could buy an island? How do the ads indicate the size of the piece of land? What price range do you find?

11.   States have areas that are protected by law from being developed, e.g., state forest lands. Look at the tourist map published by your state and locate the various kinds of protected areas. Why are these areas protected? What activities can take place there? Visit one with the class if possible or learn more about the ones nearest your town.

12.   Find examples of ways that water, air, and land can be affected or destroyed by people, animals, and nature itself. Newspapers and magazines are sources of photos of floods, fires, erosion, smoke emission, etc. Post these and indicate the problems they show.

13.   Invent an island and indicate the human and animal life that will inhabit it. What geographical features and resources must it have to support the animals and humans

you have chosen to populate it? How would your island change if it became overpopulated? *Rotten Island* by William Steig portrays this extremely well.

14. Pantomime some of the vocabulary words from the story—croak, defiant, subside, huddle, desperate, recognize, tremble.

15. The frogs constantly argued. Look in a thesaurus for other words that mean "argue." Try to add them to your everyday conversation. Make word searches of all the new words you have learned in these two activities.

16. Play "King of the Mountain" during recess. How does this relate to the story?

Related Books and References

MacDonald, Golden. *The Little Island*. New York: Doubleday, 1946.

Peet, Bill. *Wump World*. Boston: Houghton Mifflin, 1970.

Steig, William. *Rotten Island*. Boston: David Godine, 1969.

16

VOLCANOES

Hill of Fire

Thomas P. Lewis
New York: Harper and Row, 1971.

Summary

Life in the small Mexican village was quiet and peaceful until the day Pablo's father's plow sank into a hole in the cornfield. Smoke and fire rose from the earth and soon a mountain-sized volcano had been formed. Hot lava and ash poured forth destroying the tiny village and forcing the peasants to seek safety and to build a new town away from El Monstruo.

Science Topic Areas

Volcanic eruptions, Mexican village life and technology

Content Related Words

Eruption, lava, ash, magma, crater, amigo, fiesta, El Monstruo, continental drift

Activities

1. *Earthquakes* and *Eruptions of Mount St. Helens: Past, Present and Future* are two excellent pamphlets available from the Superintendent of Documents, U.S. Government Printing Office, Washington, D.C. 20402. Several weeks before the unit, have children write a letter to order them for use as a reference and source of photos.

2. Locate Paricutín volcano in the Mexican state of Michoacán.

3. Have a student look up a news magazine from the week of February 20, 1943 in the library media center or acquire one through interlibrary loan. Is this different from the way such a story would be done today, e.g., the eruption of Nevado del Ruíz in Colombia on November 13, 1985.

4. Watch a film or video of a volcanic eruption, e.g., *Born of Fire*, produced by the National Geographic Society. What materials come from the volcano? What is their source? What is the major cause of destruction to property, and to human and animal life? Identify the important parts of the volcano (see figure 16.1).

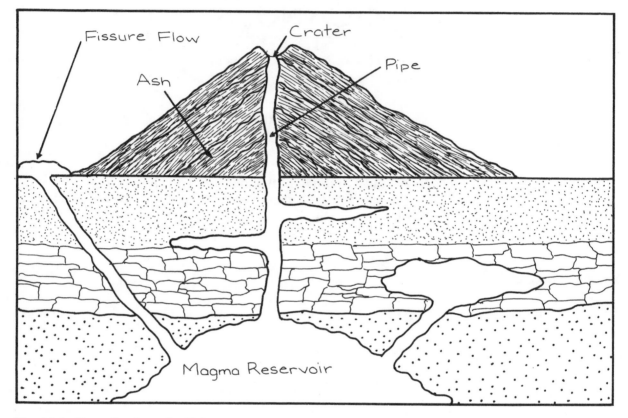

Fig. 16.1. Cross Section of a Volcano.

5. Using the *World Almanac* find the list of active volcanoes in the world. Make a tally of these by country to see which nation has the most. A color-coded bar graph could be used to show this.

6. Indicate the location of these volcanoes with pushpins or sticky dots on a world map. This arrangement of volcanoes is often called the "Ring of Fire." Why is this so? In what area of the world do most of these volcanoes lie?

7. Make a display of pictures of famous volcanoes—Mount Fuji, Mount Baker, etc. Many Pacific islands are the tops of inactive volcanoes. What characteristic features do they have in common? (Calendars are sources of excellent photos.)

8. Study a list of major volcanic eruptions as found in the *World Almanac*. Arrange these in descending order from most destructive to least destructive (i.e, number of casualties). Are any U.S. volcanoes named? Is Paricutín on the list?

9. The most recent major volcanic eruption in the continental United States was Mount St. Helens on May 18, 1980. Locate news articles in newspapers and magazines in the library media center. Compare these to *National Geographic* articles at the time.

10. Draw a series of pictures showing the formation of the volcano in *Hill of Fire* as it progressed from a hole in the field until the eruption was over. Label and sequence these events. Or have each child make a series of drawings on small paper, staple them, then flip the pages fast like a cartoon. Does the volcano seem to explode?

11. Build your own exploding volcano. To make the cone of the volcano, combine plaster mix and water, according to package directions, and pour it into a cone-shaped paper cup. When the plaster is nearly dry, turn the cup over onto a piece of foil. Trim a small section of the point of the cup away, and push a petroleum jelly-coated pencil or dowel into the point. Remove it after the plaster has hardened more. Remove the rest of the paper cup and let the plaster dry completely. Fill the "crater" with baking soda. Add a few drops of vinegar to produce the eruption. A couple of drops of food coloring can be mixed with the vinegar before putting it into the cone to produce colored effects.

12. Many volcanic eruptions can be predicted. Find out about the work and tools of a seismologist.

13. Make a bulletin board display showing a cutout section of the earth, from the surface to the core. Label the different layers (see figure 16.2) and describe them—solid, hot, etc.

14. What is a geological "fault"? What part does it play in the formation of a volcanic eruption or earthquake? Locate California's famous San Andreas fault.

15. The earth's continents were once joined. Make silhouette cutouts of the continents and see how they probably fit together in the past. Why are they separate now? What effect did that have on animals, plants, etc.? What is the meaning of the term "continental drift?"

16. Use the card catalog in the library media center to locate books on rural life in Mexico. Compare life in the Mexican village with yours in the United States. This could be done with a word chart or by using drawings or magazine photos.

17. You are visiting this Mexican town, before the explosion. Send a postcard back home telling what you like best about life in the town and what is most difficult or unfamiliar to you.

18. You are an on-the-spot reporter for the "Nightly News." Interview several different people—before, during, and after the eruption. Include news stories, feature stories, interviews.

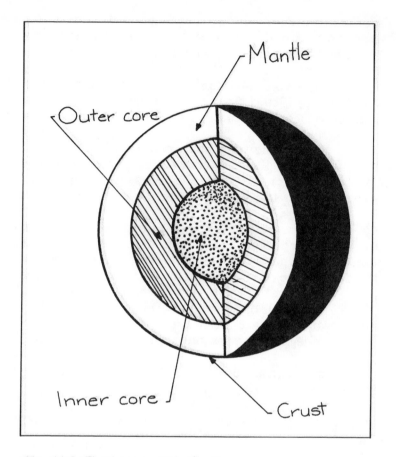

Fig. 16.2. The Layers of the Earth.

19.   Have a breakfast similar to that which the people in the story had.

Soft Tacos

1½ cups milk
3 eggs
1 cup regular flour
1 teaspoon salt
½ cup cornmeal (white or yellow)
2 tablespoons melted butter or margarine

Beat milk and eggs together in bowl. Sift in flour and salt; stir in cornmeal and melted butter. Beat until smooth. Fry on a hot, greased 7-inch frying pan, using ¼ cup batter for each taco. Tip the pan so batter spreads evenly; fry until top appears dry, then flip and brown on other side. Makes 12 tacos.

20. What is the source of cinnamon? Compare the stick and powdered forms of this spice. Sample some of the cinnamon teas available in a grocery store or make some for your breakfast.

21. Try writing some acrostics using an important word from the story as a base.

Violent
Overflowing
Lava
Cone-shaped
Ashes
Noise
Ominous

This acrostic uses phrases:

Every day it grew
Lava came from the earth
Molten rock shot into the air
Overflowing the village
Nothing was spared
Smoke and ashes everywhere
Thunderous shaking
Rumbling inside the earth
Until the village was gone
Only the hill of fire remained

22. Listen to music you would hear at a Mexican festival. What sights and activities do you imagine?

23. Listen to George Frideric Handel's *Music for the Royal Fireworks* to get an impression of how music conveys the concept of explosion.

Related Books and References

Cole, Joanna. *The Magic Schoolbus inside the Earth*. New York: Scholastic, 1988.

DuBois, William Pene. *The Twenty-One Balloons*. New York: Dell, 1984 (Chapter 10 describes the explosion of Krakatoa.)

Fiesta Mexicana (Songs and Dances of Mexico). Available as recording SP111 from Children's Book and Music Center, P.O. Box 1130, Santa Monica, CA 90406.

Findley, Rowe. "Mount St. Helens," *National Geographic*, vol. 159, no. 1 (January, 1981), pp. 640-653.

Findley, Rowe. "Mount St. Helens Aftermath," *National Geographic*, vol. 160, no. 6 (December, 1981), pp. 713-733.

Handel, George Frideric. *The Music for the Royal Fireworks*. (E.g., The Royal Philharmonic Orchestra, Yehudi Menuhin conducting. MCA Classics recording.)

National Geographic Society Educational Services. *Film and Video Catalog*. Washington, D.C.: National Geographic Society. (Published yearly)

Neilson, Virginia. *The House on the Volcano*. New York: Scholastic, 1966.

17

ROCKS

Everybody Needs a Rock

Byrd Baylor
New York: Charles Scribner, 1974

Summary

No matter who you are, you need a rock. However, there are ten rules to follow in finding the one which is perfect for you.

Science Topic Areas

Rocks, categories of rocks (not specific kinds), landforms, uses of rocks

Content Related Words

Category, texture, crystal, rock cut, erosion, glacier, fossil

Activities

1. Discuss what tools or procedures students would need to use to make a detailed observation of a rock. Try to use all five senses during the observation

2. Bring in rocks and pebbles of varying sizes, shapes, and colors. Spread them on a large table and have the students classify them. Don't give any specific directions—see what categories they discover—size, geometric shape, color, texture. Mix the rocks around and do the same thing two or three more times. Are rocks shifted to other categories?

3. Dip the stones in water. How does this change the qualities observed? This is a good time to see if rocks have an odor.

4. Have children bring in rocks they have collected from the local area or other places they have visited. Repeat the preceding activities.

5. Observe rocks under a hand lens. How does that increase the descriptive qualities? Are there more possible categories?

6. Have each child choose one rock and describe its characteristics so that a friend could select it from an array of rocks. Emphasize using terms from the classification exercises.

7. Select rocks with cracks in them. Freeze them in water, then break them with a hammer. What do you observe? Do they all break easily and evenly? What does this tell you about the effects of natural forces on rocks?

8. In what other ways does nature change rocks—erosion, glaciers, etc. Are there examples of this near you or can you find pictures illustrating this?

9. How does man change rocks—building materials, polishing and cutting them for jewelry, etc. If someone has a rock tumbler, try it out on a variety of stones. How does the appearance of the rock change? Which kinds are the first to show changes?

10. Rocks serve many purposes for people and animals. Make a chart indicating these uses and bring in magazine pictures to illustrate, e.g., hiding places for animals, old fences, building material, etc.

11. Look at your school and other large buildings in your area. Is stone one of the building materials? How many different kinds of stone were used? Was stone used for a purpose other than decoration?

12. If possible, visit a museum and study the way early cultures used stones as tools and weapons. Some museums can send a traveling exhibit of this type.

13. Have students work in pairs to make a stone artifact (see figure 17.1). Decide the purpose of the implement and the materials required to make it. Find and shape the stone, then construct the actual item. Do not allow modern tools to be used—try to do it as early man would have. (It might be necessary to substitute some items such as twine for leather strips, since these probably cannot be made or obtained by the students.)

14. Find a rock cut near the school or at a building site, or use a photo of one (see figure 17.2). What do you observe? What do the layers indicate? Why are some layers tipped or broken?

15. Are there fossils in your area? Bring in samples or use purchased ones. What different objects are fossilized? What can this tell you about an area? A book on the geology of your state could be obtained from your library media center to serve as a reference guide.

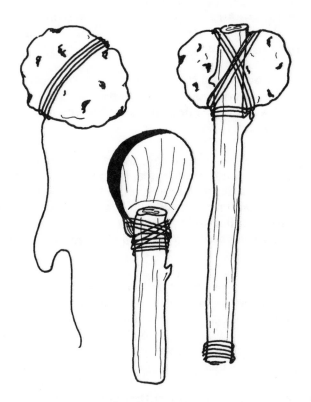

Fig. 17.1. Stone Artifacts.

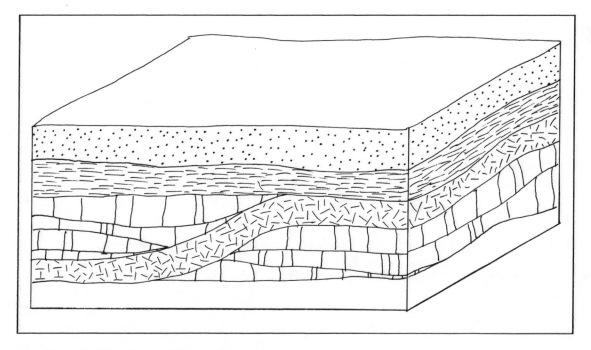

Fig. 17.2. Showing Rock Types and Layering.

16. The United States is a land of varied landforms. Watch a video of film that shows different areas of the country. How many of these scenes are a result of rocks or rock formations? What various names are given to them—mesa, butte, plateau, mountain? Which are common in your area?

17. Find photos of famous natural and carved rocks, such as the Natural Bridge in Virginia, Mount Rushmore, and Half Dome. A U.S. travel book or atlas should include these, or look through calendars. Perhaps the library media center has a file of pictures that could be borrowed.

18. Measure the volume of a rock using water displacement. Fill a glass measuring container with a specific amount of water. Immerse the rock and note the change in the level of the water. The difference between the first and second water-level reading will indicate the volume of water displaced. This method can be of use around the home to measure the volume of other solid objects. (First make sure they won't dissolve!) The principle of water displacement can be used to explain how water can be conserved by putting a brick in the toilet tank.

19. Have each student select a favorite "pet" rock from the rocks studied in class. Write a description of all the outstanding qualities this rock possesses and determine what purpose it can serve (doorstop, paperweight, or other).

20. Make jewelry, plaques, etc., from stones and pebbles, or paint larger rocks to make people, animals, or Easter eggs.

21. Grow a crystal garden. You will need these ingredients:

a glass or ceramic dish

¼ cup salt

¼ cup water

¼ cup laundry blueing

½ cup ammonia

several lumps of soft coal

Mix salt, water, blueing, and ammonia. Pour over coal which has been placed on the dish. Soak the coal thoroughly, then put a few drops of food coloring on top. Crystals will form shortly and last for several days. Compare these to the crystals in rocks.

Related Books and References

Baylor, Byrd. *Before You Came This Way*. New York: E. P. Dutton, 1969.

Cole, Joanna. *The Magic Schoolbus inside the Earth*. New York: Scholastic, 1986.

18

SOIL

Simon Underground
Joanna Ryder
New York: Harper and Row, 1976

Summary

As winter approaches, Simon the mole begins digging under the ground to build the tunnels where he will live throughout the cold months. There he eats and sleeps, safe in his home. Only as spring approaches does Simon emerge from his underground burrow.

Science Topic Areas

Soil properties, underground animal homes, seasons, winter survival

Content Related Words

Burrow, tunnel, insulator, mole

Activities

1. Obtain several soil samples (about 2 cups each) from various locations around your town. Also buy a small amount of potting soil, sand, topsoil, peat moss. Put each on a plate and compare them: smell, texture, moisture, presence of other particles. Observe each sample with a hand lens or under a microscope. What other materials do you see in the soil? Are there any organisms—living or dead?

2. Have students write descriptions of what they see in each soil sample. Compare these observations.

3. Leave a small portion of each sample out in the air. What happens? Contrast this to the sample that has been put back into a sealed container or bag.

4. Soil is porous—water will run through it. Line several funnels with a piece of filter paper and put a different kind of soil in each one. Add the same amount of water to each and see which one allows the water to penetrate first. Which is last? Make a chart indicating the time needed for each sample, and order them by name. (Make a funnel by cutting the open end off a 2- or 3-liter soda pop bottle. See figure 18.1.)

Fig. 18.1. Device for Filtering Water through Soil.

5. Mix several small sample soils with various sized stones or pebbles in a quart jar of water and shake it. Predict which objects will be at the bottom of the jar when the materials settle. What items will be in the other layers? How accurate were you?

6. Find a place where the earth has been cut exposing several layers of soil, or dig down a couple of feet and observe the layers. Notice the changes in color, texture, content, thickness of layers. Soil samples can be preserved by scattering them onto small glue-lined containers such as aspirin tins. Do this with a sample from every layer and mount them in order on posterboard. Label the soil type and characteristics of each sample.

7. Study a chart or overhead transparency of a soil profile (see figure 18.2). What types of things are found under the ground? How do these change with increasing depth. How do living plants and animals contribute to the composition of the soil? Compare this to the illustrations in the book.

8. If you know people in other parts of the country, write and ask them for a small sample of a typical soil from their area, e.g., red clay in Georgia, sandy soil in Florida, topsoil in Iowa. Compare the physical qualities and try to predict how this affects the lifestyle of the people — crops grown, amount of rainfall, etc.

9. Bring in a large shovelful of the covering of the forest floor. What items do you find? Are there any living organisms? Dry a portion of the sample and crumble it. What does this indicate about soil formation?

10. If Simon could talk, how would he explain to the other forest creatures why he goes underground for the winter? A small group of students could collaborate to play the part of Simon while other children could be nonhibernating animals who question him.

11. Animals live under the soil in winter because it has insulating qualities to keep them warm. Materials vary in their capacity to insulate, i.e., to keep things either hot or cold. Which material would keep a cup of coffee or hot chocolate warm for the longest time — plastic, paper, styrofoam, ceramic, or stoneware? Pour some hot water into cups made of the various materials and touch the side of each cup with your hand. Which becomes hottest to the touch? Which would be easiest to hold? Put fresh, hot water and a thermometer in each cup. Measure the temperature in 15 minutes and compare.

12. Glue two movable eyes onto a 1-inch pom-pom to make a "Warm Fuzzy" for use in insulation experiments. (Craft or fabric stores will carry these items.) The objective of the activity is to make a home that will keep the "Fuzzy" as warm as possible. Children may use any container or materials to do this. The insulating qualities are tested by measuring the temperature inside the container on a cold day. In warmer climates the activity is reversed, using insulation to keep the "Fuzzy" cool.

13. What commercially available items are designed to keep things hot or cold, e.g., picnic coolers? How do they work?

14. Simon has just emerged for the spring. You are a newspaper reporter interviewing him. Find out why he decided to come out, what things in nature make it obvious it is spring, why his body is shaped as it is, why he cannot see, what it is like in the tunnel all winter. (Look at the pictures to see which characteristics are most obvious — wedge-shaped nose, slit eyes, paws, fur.)

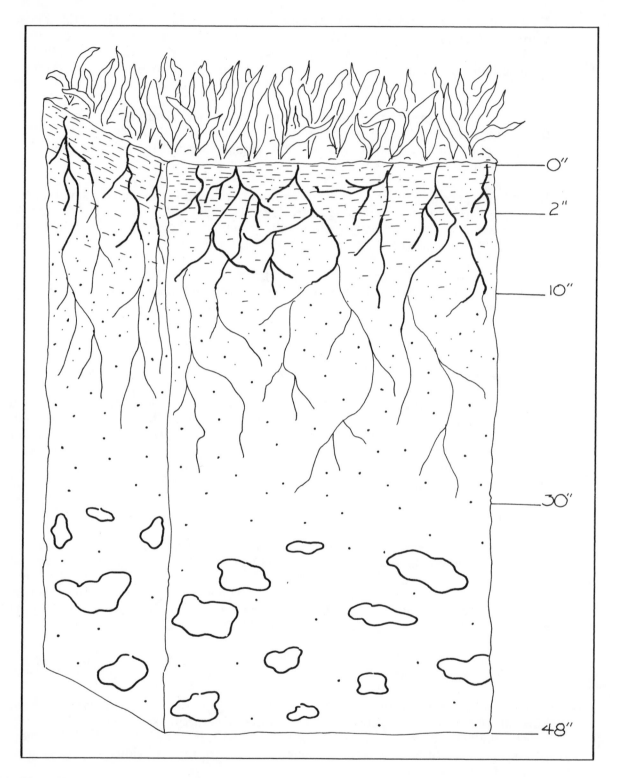

0"

2"

10"

30"

48"

Fig. 18.2. A Soil Profile

15. Obtain a variety of field guides for plant life from the library media center to learn about edible plants that grow in the forest in the spring, e.g., wild leeks, fiddlehead ferns. Gather plants native to your area and enjoy them. Be sure to get expert help and avoid mushrooms or other potentially dangerous plants.

16. Many activities mean spring for humans, e.g., Easter vacation, baseball season, cherry blossom festivals. Select one event that means the coming of spring for you. Describe the event and explain its significance.

17. Spring flowers can be made to bloom early by "forcing" them. This project, which shows the insulating properties of soil, takes 3 to 4 months. Fill a flower pot three-quarters full of good garden soil and place bulbs on the soil. Tulips, daffodils, and hyacinths work well, but should not be crowded. Cover with soil until just the bulb tops are visible, and water until thoroughly soaked. Put the pot in a dark, cool place (below 55 degrees) and water to keep soil damp. When sprouts are 2 inches long, put the pot in full sunlight. Continue watering the plant. Flowers will bloom in a few weeks.

18. Spring is a favorite topic of poets. Look in poetry anthologies for examples of serious and humorous verse.

19. Try some limericks about Simon or moles:

> Moles are nearly blind from birth,
>
> It's easy for them to live in the earth,
>
> They eat grubs while they toil,
>
> Burrowing down in the soil,
>
> But most people aren't sure of their worth.

20. Why do gardeners dislike moles intensely? What methods do they use to eliminate the moles? Have a debate. Should moles be killed because they burrow under the earth making mounds of soil on top of the lawn? What other problems do they cause for people? Do they serve any useful purpose?

21. The groundhog has a day in his honor (February 2). This is celebrated with special ceremonies and a festival in Punxsutawney, Pennsylvania. Have a special day for Simon, e.g., Mole Monday. Design activities, banners, T-shirts, bumperstickers, balloons, etc., in honor of Simon. (You must agree why he deserves this honor and follow through with it in your activities.)

22. People use tunnels under mountains and rivers. What are the problems involved in building these devices? What machines and technology must be utilized? The library media specialist can help you look for information in back issues of magazines or newspapers on projects to build tunnels, e.g., the tunnel from England to France under the English Channel. Are there tunnels of any kind in your area?

23. Listen to music about spring, e.g., "Spring Song" by Felix Mendelssohn and "Spring" (from *The Four Seasons*) by Antonio Vivaldi. Note the types of instruments used, the rhythms and tempo of the music, etc. How might this change for music about the other seasons?

Related Books and References

Larrick, Nancy. *Piping Down the Valleys Wild: Poetry for the Young of All Ages*. New York: Delacorte Press, 1985.

Mendelssohn, Felix. "Spring Song." (E.g., on *Mendelssohn's Greatest Hits*, The Boston Pops Orchestra, Arthur Fiedler conducting. RCA Victor recording.)

Ryder, Joanna. *Chipmunk Song*. New York: E. P. Dutton, 1987.

Vivaldi, Antonio. *The Four Seasons*. (E.g., Israel Philharmonic Orchestra, Zubin Mehta conducting. Deutsche Grammophone recording.)

19

LIGHTHOUSES AND OCEANS

Keep the Lights Burning, Abby

Peter and Connie Roop
Minneapolis, Carolrhoda Books, 1985
(Originally published as *Abby Burgess: Lighthouse Heroine*
by Dorothy Jones and Ruth Sargent
Camden, Maine: Down East Press, 1969)

Summary

When her father goes ashore for supplies, Abby is left in charge of her family and the lighthouse on Matinicus Rock. Her determination, dedication, and hard work enable her to keep the lamps lit throughout a storm that rages for nearly a month. This event took place in January 1856 and is recorded in Abby's own journals and elsewhere.

Science Topic Areas

Physical oceanography, lighthouses, tides, storms, navigation

Content Related Words

Puffin, lighthouse, wicks, oil lamp, concave lens, hurricane

Activities

1. Locate Matinicus Rock and Matinicus Island off the coast of Maine. What body of water surrounds them? Why is there a lighthouse there? What are the nearest mainland towns? How many miles away are they?

2. Make a list of essential items that Papa would have to bring back from town. Remember, this is a solid rock island, so everything must be carried in on a boat. Only chickens can be kept on the island.

3. Compare the pictures of Abby's room and her clothes to the items found in your room and the way you dress. What everyday essentials of your life were unknown to Abby?

4. A lightkeeper's family stayed on the rock for months at a time. Discuss how you would feel if your house were suddenly surrounded by miles of open ocean and you were to be confined there for the next six months. Also assume that you will no longer have electricity or running water. What will life be like?

5. Study the cutaway diagram of a lighthouse (figure 19.1) and see how it was used for both work and as a dwelling place. Look at the pictures of Abby's lighthouse. Using paper tubing, shoeboxes, cardboard, etc., build a model lighthouse. Lighthouses can be on a rock, on a small island, or on the shore of the ocean.

6. To show the effect of the ocean tides on land and objects, place a lighthouse model on rocks piled in a large wash basin. Add water to show that the land disappears from view as the tide comes in. Scoop out water to simulate the tide going out. Tie a small toy boat close to the lighthouse. What happens as the tide comes in and goes out? How do tides affect the life of the people on these small islands?

7. Abby tended lamps that burned oil, probably whale oil. What would happen to the oil as the temperature dropped. Put small amounts of oil we use, e.g., motor oil, salad oil, and lamp oil, into the refrigerator and some into the freezer. What do you observe? How would this complicate the process of filling the lamps? Could she solve the problem?

8. Examine a kerosene lantern or decorative oil lamp. What parts does it have? What is the difference in brightness when you place the chimney over the burning wick? What happens to the chimney after several hours of burning? How can you restore the brightness?

9. To increase the effectiveness of the lamps, there was a concave lens behind them to reflect light. Use a magnifying makeup mirror and place it behind a burning candle or lamp. What is the result? (Use a darkened room to heighten the effect.)

10. The force of the wind at sea is measured in knots. (A knot, or 1 nautical mile per hour, is about 6,000 feet, which is slightly longer than a land mile.) The following chart shows the wind speeds triggering various storm advisories as defined by the National Weather Bureau:

18-33 knots	Hazardous wind and wave conditions
34-47 knots	Gale-force winds
over 48 knots	Storm conditions
over 64 knots	Hurricane conditions

Make an approximate comparison of these speeds and driving speeds, e.g., 25 mph city traffic; 55 mph highway speed; 65 mph limited-access highway speed. Are there any other speeds you could use for comparison?

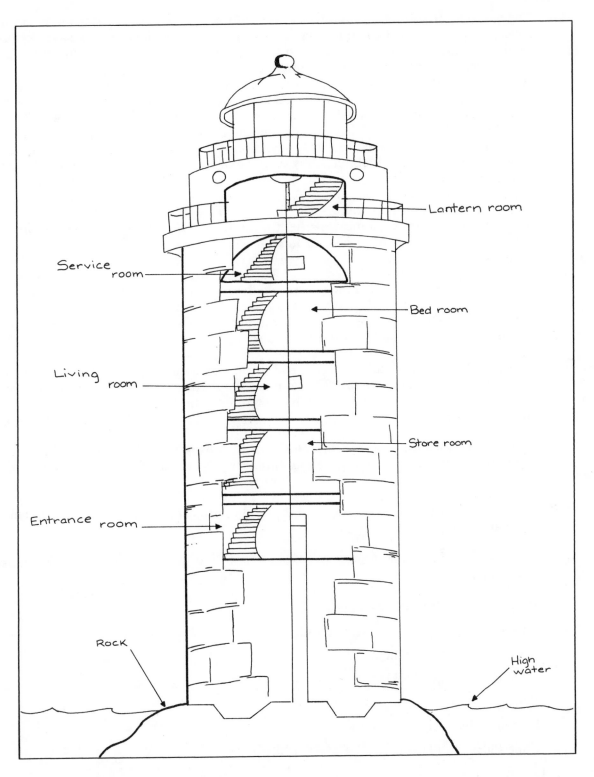

Fig. 19.1. Cutaway Diagram of a Lighthouse.

11. The sea water froze on the windows of the lighthouse. Using the freezing point for this water, and the speed of the hurricane wind, figure out how cold it may have been on Matinicus Rock. A wind chill chart in the *World Almanac* will aid you. (Note: Sea water freezes at about ten degrees fahrenheit.)

12. Pretend you are Abby and write journal entries from various times during the story, e.g., soon after Papa leaves, when the storm begins, when she lights the lamps for the first time and saves the chickens, when the supplies are nearly gone and she begins to despair, and when Papa returns. Is it possible for the library media specialist to get a copy of the original book about Abby or some of her actual journal writings through interlibrary loan?

13. If there was an award for heroism in 1856, Abby would be an excellent candidate. Write an essay or speech nominating her for this honor. Be sure to explain what she did and why you think she deserves to win.

14. How long ago did this story take place? The storm began on January 19. What is the weather generally like on that day where you live? What are the next four weeks usually like? Does the library media center have copies or microfilms of back newspapers so that you could actually see the weather report for the period covered by Abby's journal? Can you go back to the year you were born?

15. If the weather bureau predicted a very bad storm would hit your town during the night, what precautions would you take? What items should be obtained or stored if electrical and water service could possibly be interrupted? In what part of the house is it best to stay?

16. Papa's boat is called *The Puffin*. This rare bird lives few places except Matinicus Island. Look up puffins and learn about this nearly extinct species. (Puffins are not the same as penguins.)

17. Design a T-shirt or banner to publicize the need to protect puffins, since their existence is endangered.

18. There are still many lighthouses in Maine. On a road map, locate some of the most popular ones:

West Quoddy Head Light--Lubec

Bass Harbor Light--Mt. Desert Island

Rockland Breakwater Light--Rockland

Owls Head Light--Rockland

Pemaquid Point--Pemaquid Point

Portland Head Light--Portland

Cape Elizabeth (Two Lights)--Cape Elizabeth

Nubble Light--Cape Neddick

Matinicus Rock Light--Matinicus Rock

Monhegan Island Light--Monhegan Island

These are just some of the working lights in Maine. Why are there so many? How are modern lighthouses different from those of nineteenth century Maine, e.g., equipment, personnel, physical shape of building, etc.? Other areas of the country have working lighthouses, e.g., the Great Lakes. How are these like the Maine lighthouses? What is different?

19. Find pictures of lighthouses in magazine ads, photography ads, and calendars, and make a display of them. How are they similar and different? (A well-known light is the Portland Head Light in Maine, which was commissioned by George Washington as the first one in the United States.)

20. To pass the long hours, Abby's family probably sang songs of the sea and its sailors. Check the library media center for books or records of sailing songs or sea chanteys.

Related Books and References

McCloskey, Robert. *Time of Wonder*. New York: Viking Press, 1957.

Maine Publicity Bureau, 97 Winthrop Street, Hallowell, ME 04347.

Smith, Arthur. *Lighthouses*. Boston: Houghton Mifflin, 1971.

Songs and Sounds of the Sea. Washington, D.C.: National Geographic Society, 1973. (A sound recording)

Tresselt, Alvin. *Hide and Seek Fog*. New York: Lothrop, Lee and Shepard, 1965.

20

MUSSELS AND ARCTIC LIFE

The Very Last First Day
Jan Andrews
New York: Macmillan, 1986

Summary

Eva was very excited, yet apprehensive, about her first experience walking alone under the ice on the bottom of the sea. She had never gathered mussels without her mother's help, but she overcame many difficulties and problems to return with a full pan of food.

Science Topic Areas

Arctic life, oceans, tides, length of day, sea life

Content Related Words

Mussels, Arctic, tide, tundra, Inuit

Activities

1. Illustrations are a very important part of children's books. Before reading this book, have students study the cover. What predictions can they make about the life and environment of this little girl?

2. Eva's way of life is portrayed through the illustrations as well as through the words. Assign a small group of students to each of the first four pictures in the book. List all the inferences they can make about Eva's way of life from these illustrations.

3. Have the groups present their findings. As items are listed, put them on a chart indicating what is similar to modern U.S. life and what is generally unfamiliar—cornflakes would be similar, but an animal skin drying in the yard would not be.

4. Several sea animals are pictured on the ocean floor. Identify them and learn if they can be eaten by people. What other shellfish do people eat? Look at a fish store display or consult a cookbook from the library media center.

5. Get some blue mussels from a seafood store—preferably while they are still on the hair or threads that hold them together. After studying the outside, scrub the mussels under running water using a small utility brush, and pull off any remaining threads. Throw away any open shells, unless they close as you tap them. Put the mussels in a pan with a small amount of water, cover, and steam them for 5 or 6 minutes. Drain and remove the mussels from the shells. Dip into melted butter, if desired, before eating. Mussels can also be dipped in batter and deep fried or made into chowder.

6. Examine the blue mussel shell. What makes it unique? How is it similar to or different from other shells you have seen? Compare it with other shells if possible.

7. Dissect a raw mussel (see figure 20.1).

8. Mussels can be grown commercially in contained areas near the shoreline of the ocean. For more information on this project write to the Marine Advisory Service, Coburn Hall, University of Maine, Orono, Maine 04469.

9. Design a parka or boots like Eva would wear. What materials would probably be used to make her clothing?

10. Mussel shells can be used in art projects. Drill small holes in them to make mobiles. Paint pictures on them. Scratch designs on them in the manner of scrimshaw art, which was once done on whalebone. After the design has been scratched in, paint the area with india ink. Leave the ink on for a minute, then wipe it off.

11. Eva is an Inuit. These people live in the Arctic regions of the North American continent. What countries, provinces, territories, and states would this include? (*Note*: Inuits were formerly known as Eskimos.)

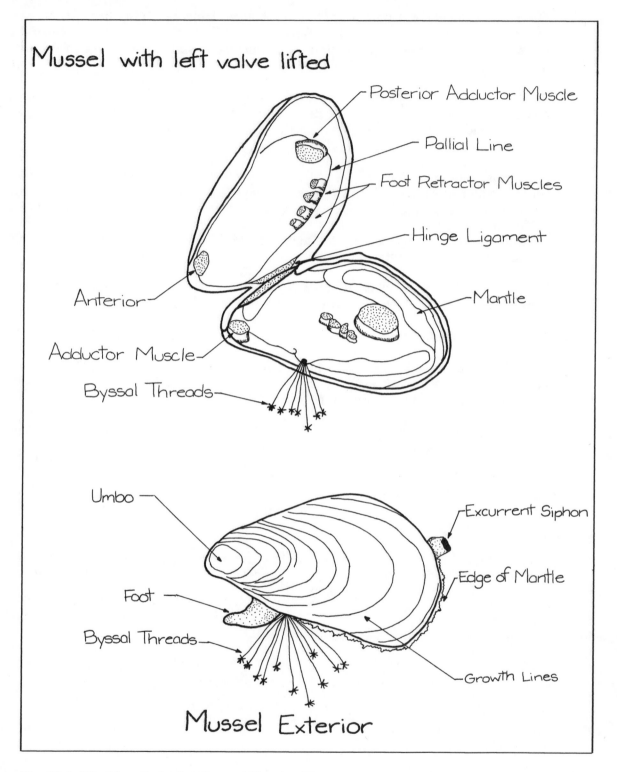

Fig. 20.1. The Mussel: An Interior and Exterior View.

12. Find words from the story that fit the blanks by Eva's name in figure 20.2. (Answer key for this puzzle is found in the Appendix.)

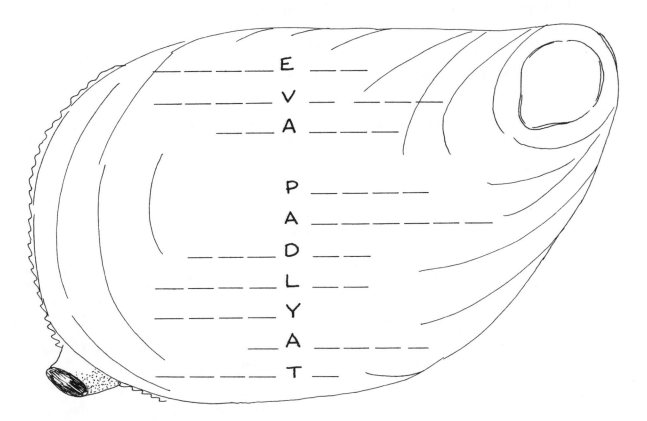

Fig. 20.2. A Puzzle for Vocabulary Review.

Clues:

(a) These people live in an isolated area near the Arctic Circle.

(b) These edible sea creatures have blue-black shells and attach themselves to rocks on the ocean floor.

(c) Eva's only means of light came from this source.

(d) These sea animals look more like beautiful moving flowers.

(e) This heavy jacket provides warmth in a cold climate.

(f) This country is one of the largest in size, but very small in population.

(g) Eva walked under the ice of this body of water.

(h) The ocean water would have this taste.

(i) The soil is frozen most of the year in this vast, treeless area.

(j) Many forms of marine plants and animals can be found here.

13. Eva has many different emotions throughout the book. Think of adjectives to describe her (excited, scared, clumsy). Write Eva's name vertically like in the puzzle, and try to fit these words around the letters of her name. Or you can think of words that begin with the ten letters of her name so that they all fit on one side of her name.

14. On a globe, find the province of Quebec in northeastern Canada. Locate Ungava Bay (south of Baffin Island) then find the Arctic Circle and the North Pole. How far is Eva's home from the Arctic Circle? From the North Pole? What is the climate like in this part of the world?

15. This area is known as the tundra. The soil temperature is below freezing for most of the year. Dig down about a foot near your home or school and measure the temperature of the soil. How would this compare to the tundra? Can there be any agriculture near Eva's home?

16. Observe the number of bodies of water, towns, and roads in the area of Ungava Bay. What does this tell you about life there— buying goods, getting food to eat, the cost of items, availability of modern conveniences, etc.?

17. What U.S. state is nearest Eva's home? What is the approximate distance from Ungava Bay to your home? How far is it to the nearest major Canadian city? Which forms of transportation could be used to get there, e.g., ship, commercial airplane, truck, auto, railroad, private plane?

18. Eva's home lies about 60 degrees of latitude north of the equator. On a globe, locate cities that are at approximately the same degree of latitude. Which one is in the United States?

19. Eva went down to gather mussels shortly after the sun came up. By the time she was finished, the moon was out. What inferences can you draw from this? Remember how far north they are. Can you figure out what time of year this is?

20. Ungava Bay empties into Hudson Strait and then into the Atlantic Ocean. This strait is frozen over for half the year, and there are icebergs in it the remainder of the year. If you wished to sail into Ungava Bay, what information would you need to have?

21. The major part of an iceberg is below the surface of the water. This is very hazardous to ships. Make an iceberg of your own. Fill an eight ounce plastic cup with water and let it freeze solid. Run warm water over the outside of the cup to loosen it. Put the block of ice into a deep bowl of water. How much of the "iceberg" can you see? Ocean water is salty. Repeat the observation with water containing several spoonfuls of salt. Is the "iceberg" more or less visible than it was in the unsalted water?

22. Ocean depth is measured in fathoms instead of feet. A map of Ungava Bay shows depth readings ranging from 5 to 84 fathoms. What would this be in feet? How does this relate to the story?

23. Eva's candles went out while she was under the ice because they were dropped and because they burned down. Candles also need air or oxygen to burn. Place identical

burning candles in holders and cover them with clear glass containers that measure a specific volume—a pint, a quart, a half gallon, a gallon. (Glass canning jars would work well.) Before you do this, predict how long each candle will burn and which will go out first. Time how long each candle burns and make a chart. Try the experiment again with candles of varying thickness but identical length. Do they all burn out at the same time?

Related Books and References

Atlas of the World. Washington, D.C.: National Geographic Society, 1981.

Cleaver, Elizabeth. *The Enchanted Caribou*. New York: Atheneum, 1985.

Nanogak, Agnes. *More Tales from the Igloo*. Edmonton, Alberta: Hurtig Publishers, 1986.

21

WATER

The Magic Schoolbus at the Waterworks
Joanna Cole
New York: Scholastic, 1986

Summary

Miss Frizzle's class was definitely not looking forward to a trip to the waterworks, but something very magical happened along the way. The students were reduced to the size of water droplets and received the best possible tour of the waterworks—from the inside!

Science Topic Areas

Water cycle, water purification, use and conservation of water

Content Related Words

Water cycle, evaporation, condensation, purification, water vapor, reservoirs

Activities

1. If possible, take a trip to the waterworks nearest you.

2. If this cannot be arranged, have a speaker from the water purification plant or the water company come to your class. Make up interview questions based on material in the book or other questions you have. Is your waterworks similar to the one Miss Frizzle's class visited?

3. Another alternative would be to take photos or a video of the closest waterworks. A narration or photo captions would be necessary to explain the process.

4. What is the source of water for your community—a lake, a river? What towns or areas must be passed as the water goes to the waterworks? Trace this on a topographic or local landform map.

5. Look at the diagram of the water cycle (figure 21.1). Trace the complete route of one drop of water. Once you know how the water cycle works, write a story of one drop of water. Remember, that drop can exist in three forms—solid, liquid and gas.

Fig. 21.1. The Water Cycle.

6. Make it rain in the classroom. An empty glass aquarium or large gallon jar can be used to make it rain indoors. Put several inches of warm water in the jar. Cover it immediately with a piece of glass or heavy plastic wrap that can be held in place by a rubber band. Put several ice cubes on top of the glass or plastic to simulate the cold air

above the earth. Place the jar in a sunny window or near a heat source. As the warm air from the water rises and meets the cold covering, what happens? How can you keep this happening? How does this relate to the picture of the water cycle?

7. Individual water cycle demonstrations can be made using clear plastic cups. Place warm water in one cup and immediately cover this with an inverted cup. The two rims should meet and be taped to keep the upper cup in place. Put ice cubes on the top cup and place it near a source of heat. Watch for clouds and rain. Is this like the diagram? (See figure 21.2.)

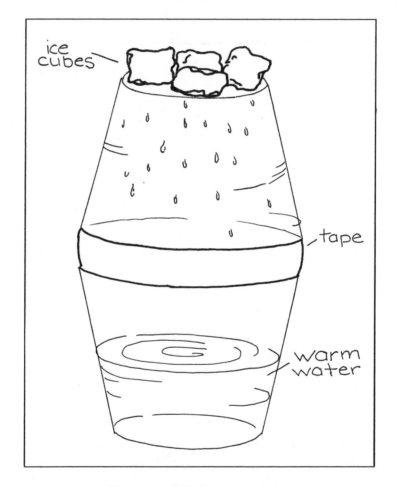

Fig. 21.2. The Water Cycle in a Cup.

8. Skim water from a running stream and from the top of a pond. Let the samples settle in separate glass containers. What do you see? Evaporate the water from the top of each container and observe what is left. (Boiling the water will speed the process.) What does this tell you about these two types of water? Will ordinary tap water be similar to either one?

9. Read your water meter at home, at the beginning and at the end of a day. How many gallons of water were used? Keep a log of the approximate amount of water that you yourself use in a day, e.g., five glasses of water, 10-minute shower, etc. What other places do you use water during a day?

10. What is conservation of water? Why is it necessary? How can it be done? Have small groups of children represent the concerns of different people, e.g., the mayor of a large city, an Arizona cotton farmer who irrigates his lands, the head of a family who must pay the water bill, a corporation president who wishes to build a 200-store super mall in southern Florida, the owner of a fishing resort in Minnesota. Write an editorial or letter to a national news magazine about the importance of wise water usage.

11. Make posters that stress the need for pure, nonpolluted water and water conservation practices.

12. Assume you have heard that the Water Quality Act of September 1965 is to be repealed or cancelled. Choose a small group to debate for and against the repeal, then have other students vote. (The *World Almanac* will contain the text of this act, as well as the Environmental Quality Index. It may be necessary to put these in simplified form before students read them.)

13. Use the circle graph in figure 21.3 to answer the following questions. Make up some questions of your own.

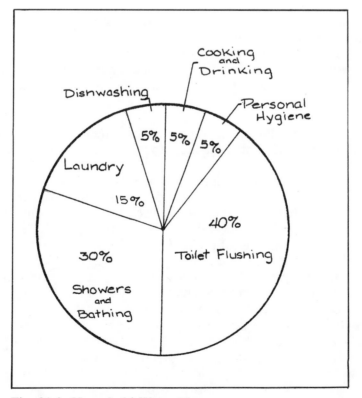

Fig. 21.3. Household Water Usage

(a) What item represents the largest daily use of water?

(b) Which accounts for the smallest amount used each day?

(c) If you combine the water needed for dishwashing, cooking, drinking, and personal hygiene, it would equal the usage for what single task?

(d) What portion of water usage is allotted to showers and bathing each day?

(e) If you wanted to conserve water or cut the cost of your bill, what item would you probably try to change? How could you do it?

14. In what areas would it be most difficult to cut down water use? Why?

15. Learn to read your family's water bill — number of gallons used, cost, number of days in a billing period, date due, taxes applied, how to inquire about poor service or an inaccurate statement, etc.

(a) Compare the usage and cost of water service at various times of the year, or every month if the receipt is available. Make a line graph of these figures.

(b) Compare the usage and cost in one particular month for various families — those with an infant and other small children, those with several teenagers, an older person living alone, etc.

16. It has been a very dry season and your town's water supply is rapidly being depleted. You are members of the town council and must decide on what measures can be taken to conserve water and how to enforce these temporary restrictions. What are the first restrictions you make? What are the additional ones? How do you decide this? What is the penalty for breaking these rules? What is the alternative when the water supply is totally gone?

17. Write a news article explaining these conservation measures. You must convince people of the need for this and that what they do will actually help alleviate the problem.

18. Nearly three-fourths of the human body is composed of water. The amount of the earth's surface covered by water is also about three-fourths of the total area. To see this visually, cut an apple in half, then divide each half evenly. Three pieces represent the amount of water in the body or on the earth. Continue cutting to find how much usable land there is. Cut one-quarter of the apple in half. Set aside one side as representing all the land that is too dry, hot, cold, or wet for people. You have one-eighth of the apple left. Cut it into four pieces. Take only one piece (one-thirty-second of the apple) and this is the total amount of land that can be used for farming. One tiny slice off this last piece represents all the drinkable water of this area. What inferences can you make from this activity?

19. Crossword Puzzle (figure 21.4). (An answer key for this puzzle is found in the appendix.)

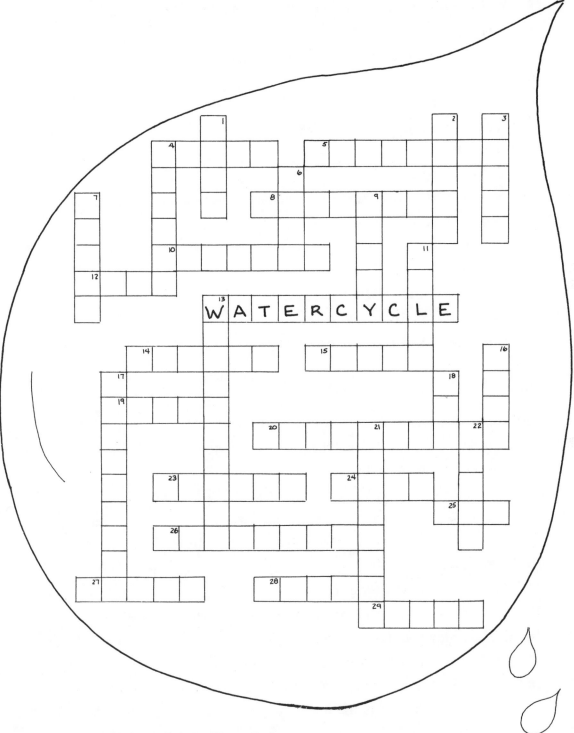

Fig. 21.4. Crossword Puzzle for the Water Cycle.

Across

4 Worn or broken pipes must be fixed to stop this waste

5 It helps prevent cavities

8 The force of water as it moves through pipes

10 Frozen polar water

12 A material used to filter water

14 A device to strain out bits of dirt

15 Water droplets high in the sky

19 An invisible gas

20 Disease-causing chemicals that are dumped into water

23 Process to clean water

24 It is added to water to form globs of dirt and mud

26 A place where water is stored

27 Strong ones need good food and water

28 Tanks used to mix and settle water

29 Three-quarters of it is covered by water

Down

1 These large water carriers run under the city streets

2 Concrete, metal, or plastic tubes that carry water

3 They cause disease and sickness

4 Water exists in this form, as well as in solid and gas form

6 The children were turned into water this size

7 Less than 1 percent of the earth's water is this kind

9 Ocean water tastes like this

11 Water turned to ice, for example

13 Dirty or impure water becomes safe and usable here

16 Cold air moves in this manner

17 To change from a liquid to a gas

18 When heated, water turns into this form of matter

21 It kills germs that are in the water

22 Large containers for storing water

20. Find some famous sayings about water, e.g., "Water, water everywhere and not a drop to drink."

21. Listen to George Frideric Handel's *Water Music* suite as you work.

Related Books and References

Aardema, Verna. *Bringing the Rain to Kapiti Plain*. New York: Dial Press, 1981.

Handel, George Frideric. *Suite from The Water Music*. (E.g., The Royal Philharmonic Orchestra. Yehudi Menuhin conducting. MCA Classics recording.)

Shulevitz, Uri. *Rain, Rain Rivers*. New York: Farrar, Straus, 1969.

22

ASTRONOMY AND OUTER SPACE

Space Songs
Myra Cohn Livingston
New York: Holiday House, 1988

Summary

The heavenly bodies are described in poetry that appeals to both the intellect and the emotions. The awesome facts about this much-studied, but little-known frontier, give us clues to the meaning of the vastness that surrounds us. Still, outer space has relinquished few of its many secrets.

Science Topic Areas

Outer space, heavenly bodies, man-made space objects

Content Related Words

Moon, sun, planets, asteroids, meteorites, comets, constellations, satellites, black hole, magnet, void, sphere, orbit, crater

Activities

General

1. A visit to a planetarium or museum space display is an excellent way to introduce or wrap up the unit. If this cannot be done, obtain some of the excellent videos on outer space. Knowledge of this area is gained mainly by observation and inferential reasoning, rather than by first-hand experience.

2. Have students locate newspaper and magazine articles in the library media center about discoveries or exploration in outer space, the U.S. space program, and celestial occurrences, e.g., eclipses, comets, meteor showers, etc. The library media center specialist may have filmstrips or videos about the U.S. space program.

3. Keep track of technical words from this unit and use them to make a large crossword puzzle as a final project.

4. Find poetry about outer space in other books or anthologies. Compare it to the works in *Space Songs* for content, descriptive images, and the actual shape of the poem.

5. Choose one of the topics in the book and describe it figuratively or in a "shape" poem. You may need to look up additional facts on your topic.

6. Design a rocket or other means of transportation that could be used in outer space. Paper cups, plates, tubes, etc., make excellent construction materials.

7. In outer space, your weight would change according to the gravitational pull. Determine your weight on:

   (a) the moon—one-fifth your earth weight

   (b) the sun—thirty times your earth weight

   (c) Venus—three-fourths your earth weight

   (d) Mars—one-third your earth weight

   (e) Jupiter—two and one-half times your earth weight

The Moon

1. Using a detailed map of the moon as a guide, make a papier mâché moon, complete with craters and seas. This can be done three-dimensionally using a large beach ball or balloon as a form.

2. For one month, observe the moon each night and keep a log. Make sketches of how it looks, along with a brief written description. On some nights, observe the moon several times. How does its relative size and color appear to change? Is it ever visible during the day? What time does the moon "rise"? Are there nights you cannot see the moon? Why?

3. Shine a flashlight or slide projector on a large ball. One side of the ball will be illuminated, like a full moon. (See figure 22.1.) As children move to the side of the ball, less of the light will be seen and the moon will appear to become a crescent. By moving from one side of the ball, across the front of it to the other side, it is possible to observe the phases of the moon. Discuss why this happens.

Fig. 22.1. Phases of the Moon Simulation.

The Stars

1. Learn the names and identifying patterns of several major constellations. Look for them on a clear night. The *World Almanac* or other reference book will list many constellations. Many people know the signs of the zodiac.

2. To know which stars are visible in your area every month, check "Evening Skies" and "Sky Calendar," which appear in each issue of *Science and Children*, published by the National Science Teachers Association. Your library media center may subscribe to this publication. Compare the sky charts for different months.

3. Make a constellation gazer using an empty shoe box. With a pin, poke holes in the form of a constellation in a sheet of black paper. Cut a rectangular slot in one end to hold the constellation. A hole for a flashlight can be cut in the opposite end of the box. With the lights off, project the image on a light-colored wall. (See figure 22.2.)

Fig. 22.2. Constellation Gazer.

4. Invent your own constellation and make up a story to accompany it.

5. The temperature of a star can be told by the color of its burning gases:

Blue-white equals 22,000 degrees F

White equals 19,000 degrees F

Yellow equals 10,000 degrees F

Orange equals 8,000 degrees F

Red equals 5,000 degrees F

What color would the following stars be? Rank them in order from the hottest to the least hot. Where does our sun fit on this list?

Rigel – 22,000 degrees

Betelgeuse – 5,000 degrees

Vega – 19,000 degrees

Sun – 10,000 degrees

Aldebaran – 7,500 degrees

Spica – 22,000 degrees

Procyon – 13,500 degrees

Antares – 5,000 degrees

Capella – 10,000 degrees

Sirius – 19,000 degrees

Canopus – 13,500 degrees

Arcturus – 7,500 degrees

The Planets

1. Make a solar system on a bulletin board display, or use various sized spheres to make a free hanging solar system across the room. Arrange the planets in the proper order, starting with those closest to the sun. Commercially made planet mobiles are also available in educational supply stores or from mail order houses, e.g., The Nature Company, Box 2310, Berkeley, CA 94702.

2. Have the children stand on the playground according to the distance of the planets from the sun. Let 1 inch equal 1 million miles. Mercury is 36 million miles from the sun, so that student would stand 36 inches from the sun. Other distances are: Venus – 62 million miles, Earth – 93 million miles, Mars – 141 million miles, Jupiter – 482 million miles, Saturn – 856 million miles, Uranus – 1,721 million miles, Neptune – 2,656 million miles, Pluto – 3,660 million miles. Now, sequence the children by the size of the planet each represents. How does this compare with their previous order based on distance from the sun?

3. Children can make their own solar systems by hanging different sized styrofoam balls from a plastic or styrofoam plate or coat hanger.

4. Divide the class into eight groups – one for each planet, except Earth. Look up facts about each planet, then invent a creature which could live there. A written and visual description should be done.

5. Each planet has an astronomical symbol. Using these, create a secret code by which you could communicate with others. (See figure 22.3.)

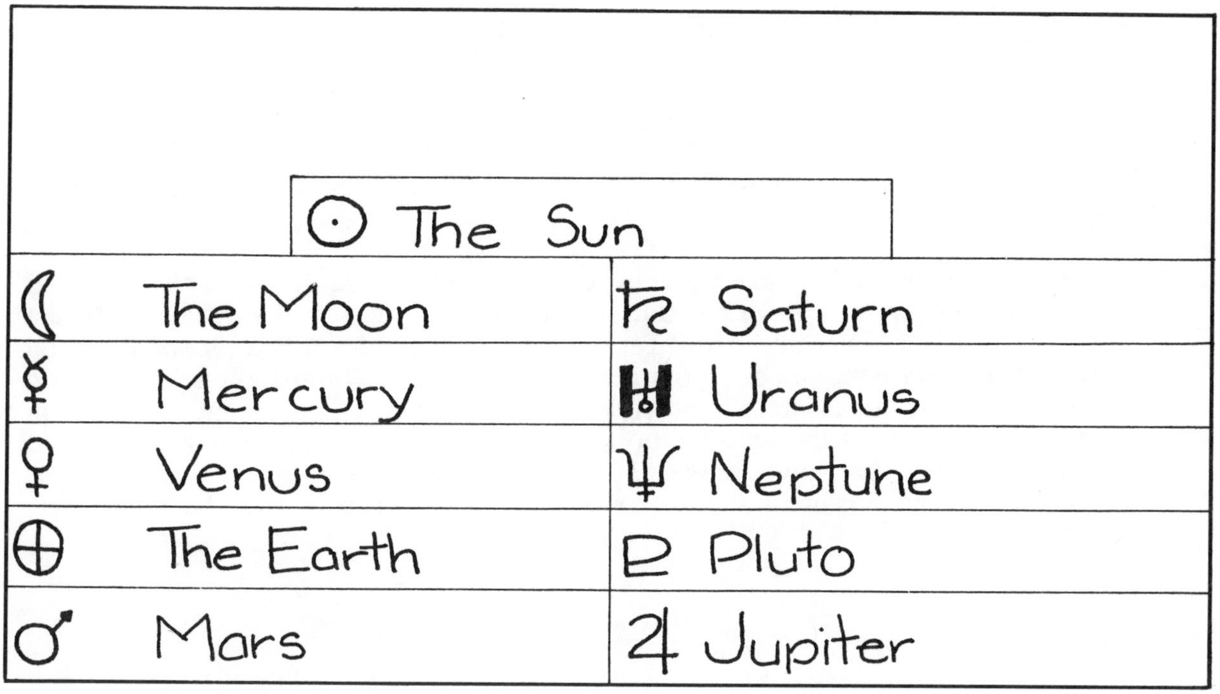

☉ The Sun	
☾ The Moon	♄ Saturn
☿ Mercury	♅ Uranus
♀ Venus	♆ Neptune
⊕ The Earth	♇ Pluto
♂ Mars	♃ Jupiter

Fig. 22.3. Astronomical Signs and Symbols.

6. *The Planets* by Gustav Holst is an exciting symphonic description of seven of the planets. Note the ways, using music, he differentiates between the planets. (Pluto had not been discovered when this was written and Earth was not included.)

Artificial Satellites

1. Artificial satellites are manufactured objects that orbit the earth to, among other things, help improve our communication system and knowledge of the weather. Check to see if your town has one of the following facilities. Visit it or get printed material about it to study.

    *   a business that sells satellite dishes for television reception

    *   a weather bureau that uses satellite photos to predict weather

    *   a television studio that sends programs over satellites

- a newspaper office that receives its overseas and distant stories by satellite

- a telephone company that uses satellites for long distance phone hookups

- a university or business that engages in teleconferencing

The Sun

1. Watch a film or video of the sun, e.g., *The Sun: Earth's Star*, produced by the National Geographic Society.

2. To observe the sun safely, make a pinhole camera (see figure 22.4). Cut a piece 2 inches square from the end of a large box and tape aluminum foil over the opening. Make a small pinhole in the center of the foil. Tape an index card inside the box, opposite the foil end. Outdoors, place the box over your head with the pinhole towards the bright sun. *Do not look at the pinhole.* Carefully observe the image of the sun on the index card. You should see the colors of the sun, and possibly even solar flares. Describe in writing and through visual arts what you have seen. (*Under no conditions should you look directly at the sun.* The pinhole camera allows you to safely see a reflection of the sun and its activity.)

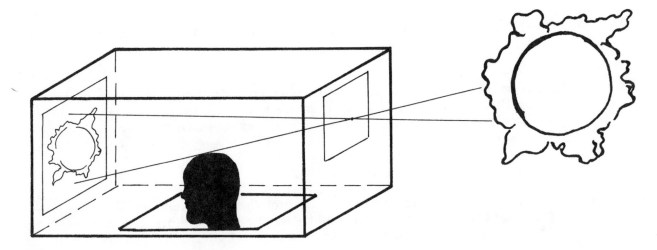

Fig. 22.4. The Pinhole Camera.

3. Solar flares shoot out from the edge of the sun. With finger paints or water colors, create your own flares using yellows and reds.

4. Make "sun tea." Place four tea bags and one quart of water in a clear, closed container. Place the bottle in the sun for several hours until the tea has brewed. Serve it over ice if you wish.

5. The sun is the source of energy for growth and life, but it can also cause harm. Look at various suntan lotions and sunscreen products in the drug store. What ingredients are most commonly found in them? Each container should bear a number to indicate its protective qualities. What do these numbers represent? Which products would give the best protection?

Meteors

1. Meteors are often called "shooting stars" or "falling stars." What are some legends or folklore connected with these objects?

2. Meteors and the core of the earth are both made of iron. Meteors often become magnetized as they pass through the earth's magnetic field. Make your own magnet by taking a small piece of iron such as a nail, and rubbing it on a magnet. Try to pick up small metal objects like paper clips with the nail. What do you observe?

3. Consult newspapers in your library media center for announcements of upcoming meteor showers. These usually occur on January 3, April 20, May 1-11, July 28-August 4, August 9-13, October 19-23, November 14-17, and December 11-13. Try to observe these. A telescope or binoculars may be of use if the meteors are not traveling too fast.

4. In the library media center, locate a book on astronomy or meteors. What is the difference between a meteor and a meteorite? Is it possible to use the words interchangeably?

Comets

1. Comets resemble a moving star that has a tail. They were cause for great alarm in ancient days. Write a story as if you were one of the leaders of these early people. You do not understand what comets are, but must make up an explanation that will resolve the fears of your people.

2. Why is Halley's Comet so famous? When will it appear again? How old will you be? Can you find names of other comets that reappear regularly? (Consult Isaac Asimov's *How Did We Find Out about Comets*?)

Asteroids

1. What keeps asteroids in orbit? Where did they originate? Look up the asteroids mentioned in *Space Songs* (Eros, Icarus, Vesta, and Flora) and other asteroids. What do their names represent?

2. Design an asteroid using a potato and painting it as you wish. Suspend it from the ceiling along with your solar system.

3. "Avoid the Asteroid!" In the gymnasium or on the playground students pretend to be asteroids by crouching down. They are allowed to move their bodies, but cannot actually walk around. Select several students to "navigate" from one end of the room to the other without being hit by an asteroid.

Related Books and References

Asimov, Isaac. *How Did We Find Out about Comets?* New York: Walker, 1975.

Blocksma, Mary, and Dewey Blocksma. *Easy to Make Space Ships That Really Fly.* New York: Simon and Schuster, 1983.

Holst, Gustav. *The Planets.* (E.g., The Boston Symphony Orchestra, Seiji Ozawa conducting. Philips recording.)

National Aeronautics and Space Administration 1958-1983 (twenty-fifty anniversary booklet). Superintendent of Documents, U.S. Government Printing Office, Washington, D.C. 20402. (Excellent source of photos of and from outer space.)

National Geographic Atlas of the World. Washington, D.C.: National Geographic Society, 1981. (Contains detailed maps of the solar system and heavenly bodies, plus other astronomical information.)

National Geographic Educational Services. *Film and Video Catalog.* Washington, D.C.: National Geographic Society. (Published yearly).

National Science Teachers Association, 1742 Connecticut Avenue, NW, Washington, D.C. 20009.

Zim, Herbert, and Robert Baker. *Stars: A Guide to the Constellations, Sun, Moon, Planets and Other Features of the Heavens.* New York: Golden Press, 1956.

Part IV
PHYSICAL SCIENCE

23

THE EYE, VISION, AND OPTICS

Spectacles
Ellen Raskin
New York: Atheneum, 1968

Summary

Iris sees things around her house in most peculiar ways—she thinks a kitten on the couch is a bulldog, children lined up in class resemble a caterpillar, Aunt Fanny appears to be a dragon, and even the optometrist becomes a blue elephant. After a visit to the optician, Iris is fitted for glasses and sees the world as it should be seen.

Science Topic Areas

The eye, vision, corrective lenses, eye examinations

Content Related Words

Spectacles, eye glasses, contact lenses, prescription, optician, optometrist, iris, concave, convex

Activities

1. Put a few drops of water on a sandwich bag or a small piece of plastic wrap. Move this around over printed material. What happens to the words? If the drops run together is there a change?

2. Mix a packet of unflavored gelatin with ½ cup water and put it in three or four tightly closed plastic sandwich bags to congeal. (Use one bag inside another for strength.) Place the bag on any printed material such as words in a book. The clear gelatin will change shape as the lens in the human eye does, and magnify the item underneath it.

3. Look at a set of eyeglass lenses. Examine the thickness, the shape, and the color of the lens. Hold them 12 to 18 inches in front of you. If objects are magnified, it is a convex lens to correct farsightedness. If objects seem smaller, it is a concave lens to correct nearsightedness. Correction for astigmatism is evident if objects change shape when the lens is rotated.

4. All eyeglass lenses are not made from the same material. What are the advantages and disadvantages of the different alternatives?

5. Compare a plastic or paper eye model to a camera and its parts. Have the class take a few snapshots around the school and get them developed to post on the bulletin board.

6. Organize eye exams for your class.

7. Take a field trip to the optometrist or optician, or visit the office and have an assistant show you the equipment and facilities. Write a language experience story about the visit.

8. Use magnifying glasses, magnification boxes or Fresnel lenses to look at items around the classroom or outside. Insects, small plants, and soil can be especially interesting.

9. Have a person who wears contact lenses explain how they are different from regular eye glasses—comfort level, care of lenses, cost advantages, disadvantages, etc.

10. A grandparent or older person who has had cataracts removed might explain how this is done. Children can make up interview questions before the visit.

11. Learn the difference among optometrist, optician and ophthalmologist by doing a short skit of a child going for an eye exam—costumes and props are very important!

12. Make up an eye chart for younger children using little pictures or symbols as means of word identification.

13. Have children sit through a language class blindfolded. Discuss their reactions and put these feelings on the board. Is there a wide range of emotions or do children react the same?

14. A visually impaired student will enter the class in a few days. Have students spend some time maneuvering with blindfolds and a stick or cane before they come. Write about the experience telling problems you had, ways you had to compensate, etc. How will this help you understand and assist the new student?

15. When light beams through bottles of water or a prism, the eye sees a rainbow (see figure 23.1). What are the colors of the rainbow or spectrum? How are rainbows produced in nature?

16. After studying about rainbows, learn some rainbow songs—"Over the Rainbow" from *The Wizard of Oz*, "The Rainbow Connection" from *The Muppet Movie*.

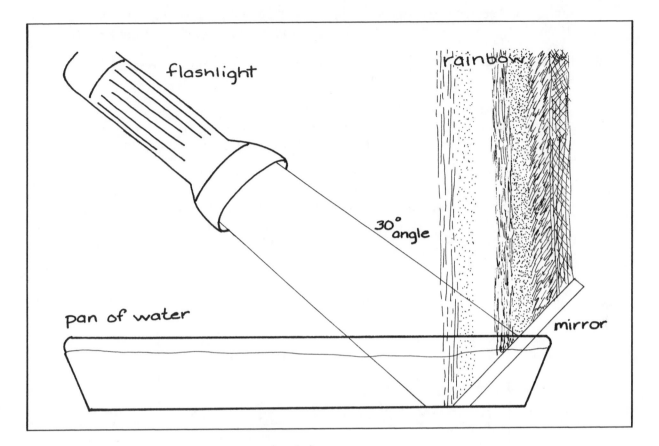

Fig. 23.1. A Spectrum or Rainbow Produced Indoors.

17. Write haiku poems about the sights of nature and the world. The teacher could begin the lesson by reading poems that are intense in their visual imagery.

18. Use magazine photos from your library media center to make a display showing people wearing glasses. What image do these people give? Are there famous entertainers or politicians shown? What eye care products do you find advertised in magazines?

19. Make a mystery box. In it, place an unknown item that will make a distinctive sound when the box is manipulated, e.g., a pine cone, some rice. Each child shakes the box. Record the observations or guesses made about the identity of the object. Stress recording of details. Give several children a turn each day. Record the results, but don't tell if anyone is correct until all have a chance to guess.

20. Discuss good eye care and list examples, such as the use of protective gear in sports, playground safety, and avoidance of dangerous toys and pointed objects.

21. Consult with your library media center specialist to locate information about services for the visually impaired. You may find directories of services very helpful. What

services and educational opportunities are available to those who are visually impaired or blind, e.g., special schools, guide dogs, talking books, home-delivered meals, etc.?

22. Design eyeglass frames for each child to make out of thin cardboard — make them humorous, intelligent, glamorous, etc.

23. To see three-dimensional effects, bring in old viewmasters or stereoscopes. Have someone show ways of drawing pictures that have dimension. Or make three-dimensional objects, e.g., cardboard castles from paper towel rolls, empty tissue boxes, cereal cartons, etc.

24. In a paper grocery bag, make a cutout section about 8 inches square. Cover this with waxed paper, colored cellophane, or theater gel and secure it with masking tape. (See figure 23.2.) The bags are placed over the students' heads to show them how other people's perception of the world is different. (Do not allow students to put plastic bags near their faces.)

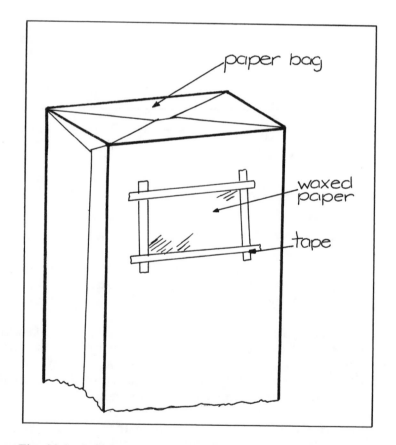

Fig. 23.2. A Sight Distortion Bag.

25. Play tag or have a scavenger hunt while wearing these paper bags. This also emulates the poor vision that many animals have and shows how difficult it is for them to find food. Write language experience stories about the simulation.

Related Books and References

Brighton, Virginia. *Five Secrets in a Box*. New York: E. P. Dutton, 1987.

Brown, Marc. *Arthur's Eyes*. Boston: Little, Brown, 1979.

24

SHADOWS AND LIGHT

Shadows

Blaise Cendrars, translated by Marcia Brown
New York: Macmillan, 1982

Summary

This African folktale personifies the shadow as a creature of both day and night, and good and evil. Shadow is a living being of great importance to the people in this tale.

Science Topic Area

Formation and change of shadows, light sources, movement

Content Related Words

Shadow, shaman, mute

Activities

1. Let the children make hand-shadow animals on a screen, using the slide projector as a source of light. How many different animals can they create? Do they move?

2. Place a large piece of light-colored paper on the wall and have each student stand for a profile drawing. Cut out the light paper and use it as a pattern to duplicate the profile on a piece of black paper. Mount the black profile on a backing sheet. Can students identify one another's silhouettes?

3. Discuss where and when shadows are found. What circumstances make it possible for a shadow to appear or disappear? Use a portable light source to make shadows around the room. How would you define or explain "shadow"?

4. What sources of indoor lighting did people use before electricity? Bring in some of these, e.g., kerosene lamp, camp lantern, candles. How are the shadows different from those in an electrically lighted room? Darken the room as much as possible to obtain the greatest effect. How would life be different if you used these methods, e.g., no nighttime sporting events.

5. Set up a sundial in the school yard on a clear, bright day. Fasten a pole to the ground in a spot where other objects will not cast a shadow on it. Indicate which direction is "north." Every hour, mark the length of the shadow and the time of day with chalk. (See figure 24.1.) Ask volunteers to continue doing this until the sun goes down. Examine the lengths of the lines. When are shadows shortest? longest? Is there symmetry to the lines? How did people use this method to tell time? What are the disadvantages? Will the shadows be the same at all times of the year? Are they the same in every part of the world?

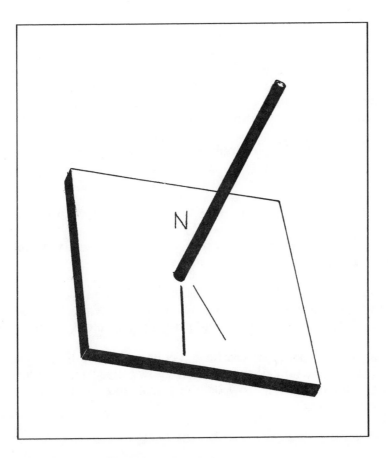

Fig. 24.1. A School Yard Sundial.

6. The shadow in this folktale is personified, or treated as if it were a person. Why do you think this is so? Why was this story told by the shaman only on certain evenings? Are there times when we speak of objects in nature as if they had human qualities, e.g., the man in the moon.

7. What adjectives does the author use to describe the shadow? To what senses does he appeal? What mood does he set? Is this a common association with shadows? Can you think of other stories or tales in which shadows are similarly treated?

8. This book is rich in action words that describe what the shadow does — prowls, spies, etc. Find all these verbs and act them out or use them to tell stories.

9. Poets like Robert Louis Stevenson have written famous poems about shadows. Ask your library media specialist to help you locate a variety of poems about shadows. Do those poems speak of the shadow in human terms as the book does? Do they contain scientific facts or concepts?

10. Try your own shadow poetry. This formula will produce a diamond-shaped work:

    Line 1 — write a noun

    Line 2 — write two adjectives describing the noun

    Line 3 — write three participles (ending in -ed or -ing) to attribute action to the noun.

    Line 4 — write four nouns relating to the subject (two nouns may have opposite meanings from the other two)

    Line 5 — write three participles indicating change or development of the subject

    Line 6 — write two adjectives continuing the idea of line 5

    Line 7 — write a noun that is opposite in meaning to the noun in line 1

    This works well as a group activity to get started, especially if the role of the word is emphasized and not its grammatical name.

11. Make a class booklet about shadows. Have each student contribute a sentence and an illustration to indicate what shadows mean to them, e.g., "Shadows are places to tell ghost stories." This could be accompanied by a picture of children around a camp fire.

12. Your library media specialist may have a collection of radio programs from the 1940s and 1950s. Listen to a tape of the old radio show called "The Shadow." Why is the main character given this name? How do the words and sound effects create a mood of suspense and mystery?

13. Design and make a shadow mask like the ones worn in the story.

14. Cut out two identical silhouettes of an object — one in black and one in any other color. Put the black one underneath but leave about ½ inch showing on two sides. Notice the three-dimensional effect that is produced by this "shadow." Make a bulletin board scene using several cutouts. (The scene of the men going to war illustrates this.)

15. Make a shadow theater and figures to produce your own original or adapted story. Stage the presentation in the library media center on parents' night or for a schoolwide gathering.

    Puppets—cut black silhouette figures. These may have separate arms, legs, and head which are joined to the body with brass fasteners. Attach the figures to soda straws or popsicle sticks.

    Theater—cut a stage opening in the front of a box. Remove the back of the box and tape a piece of thin tissue or tracing paper over it. The opening on the front of the box remains uncovered. (See *The Enchanted Caribou* by Elizabeth Cleaver for directions.)

    Production—have one student sit behind the back of the box and shine a flashlight onto the tracing paper. Another student sits next to him or her and manipulates the puppets behind the screen. The audience will see a shadow effect in the stage opening. (The children should be lower than the table on which the box is placed so that their shadows do not interfere with those of the puppets.)

16. Invent some "shadow dancing" routines. Have two children, one behind the other, do identical parallel movements. The child in back, who is the shadow, might wear dark clothes to heighten the effect.

Related Books and References

Cleaver, Elizabeth. *The Enchanted Caribou*. New York: Atheneum, 1985.

Larrick, Nancy. *Piping Down the Valleys Wild: Poetry for the Young of All Ages*. New York: Delacorte Press, 1985.

25

SHAPES

The Secret Birthday Message
Eric Carle
New York: Harper and Row, 1986

Summary

A secret message sends Timmy hunting for distinctively shaped clues. At the end of the search he finds a very special birthday present.

Science Topic Area

Geometric shapes, diagrams, following directions

Content Related Words

Circle, square, rectangle, triangle, oval

Activities

1. Make a card with a name of your favorite shape on one side and the outline of that shape on the other side. Then make a drawing using that shape as the focal point of the artwork. Gather the shape cards from all the students and try to match the cards with the drawings. Hang the matched cards together.

2. Look at one wall of the classroom and name or sketch all the various shapes that you see, e.g., square storage compartments, round clock, etc. Which shapes are most common? Are some superimposed on others, such as a round clock in a square frame? Are there some common shapes you don't find?

3. Geometric shapes are found in nature—rocks, shells, plant stems (cross section). Bring in examples.

4. Study a picture of a big-city skyline. What shapes do you see? Cut construction paper into these shapes and make your own city.

5. Traffic signs are often identified by their shapes as well as the words on them. Match the shape and the message (see figure 25.1).

Fig. 25.1. Traffic Signs.

6. Write down other words that appear on traffic signs. How many words can you find on square signs, on rectangular signs, on round ones, etc.?

7. Go to the library media center and locate pictures of traffic signs. They are often provided on maps of states or provinces and in travel magazines. Many shapes on traffic signs are silhouettes. Sometimes they show a red circle and a slash across them to show something is not allowed, e.g., a car with the red circle and slash means "No Parking." Create some of your own signs to help remind students of school rules, e.g., a foot or shoe with the red symbol could mean "no running in the halls."

8. Make a "Concentration" or "Memory" game. Have several pairs of cards that show common shapes or silhouettes. Mix them up, turn them face down, and allow a student to turn over two cards at a time. If the pair matches, the player may take them. If not, the cards are turned face down again and the next student tries to find a match. The one with the most pairs at the end wins. Be sure the winner can name all the shapes.

9. Alone or with a partner, pantomime or use your body to form a shape. Can your friends guess which one you are?

10. "Who Am I?" Describe things that have a certain shape. How many clues must you give before you are identified?

11. Place objects on the overhead and project their shapes onto a screen. Can students guess what they are? Use items such as a football, a carrot, a pine cone. (Shield the sides of the projector so objects can't be seen except on the screen.)

12. Blindfold some students and have them sit with their backs to the class. Hand them an object, such as a seashell. As they manipulate the item, have them think of descriptive words. Record these on the board. Class members must try to identify the article from the description. The words on the board can be used to create some poetry about the object.

13. Hide several large cutouts of common shapes around the room. Divide the class into small groups and give each a list of clues to help find their shape. Each group could also have a floor plan of the room and mark where they find each clue. The pathway they followed can then be plotted.

14. What are the names of the shapes that make up a tangram puzzle? (See figure 25.2.) Use the pieces of a tangram puzzle to form an object, then trace the item on construction paper, cut it out, and mount it. Can anyone figure out how the pieces fit together to form a square?

15. Write an adventure/mystery story using your own choice of shapes as clues. Have other students try to solve the puzzle. Make a booklet of your story. The shape of the cover and pages can be an outline of your main character, e.g., a bear, a child, a ladybug.

16. Write a story about a specific shape or an item that represents a certain shape, e.g., a quarter. This could be a group story in which someone starts the adventure and passes it along for the next person to add an episode or solve the problem and set up another incident.

17. Make leaf rubbings or preserve leaves between sheets of clear adhesive film. Classify the leaves by their shapes.

18. Make mosaic pictures by pasting squares of colored paper (about ½ to 1 inch in size) onto another sheet of construction paper or light cardboard. These can be done on both sides of a cutout to form mobiles or holiday hangings.

Fig. 25.2. Tangram Puzzle.

19. Modern art often depends on geometric shapes as an important element in the work. Study some plates from an art book, from your library media center, then try your hand at being a modern artist. Pictures could be drawn, painted, or composed of pieces of paper cut into shapes. Tissue-paper shapes can be layered or partially superimposed on one another for exciting effects in the style, for example, of Wassily Kandinsky's *Layers*.

20. Share expressions we use that include the word shape, e.g., "staying in shape," and "shape up." What do these mean?

21. A hopscotch diagram is a series of geometric shapes (see figure 25.3). Identify these. Can you make other arrangements or use different shapes to create your own hopscotch board?

22. Try to make up your own shape song or write words that fit a tune you all know, e.g., "Old MacDonald Had a Farm."

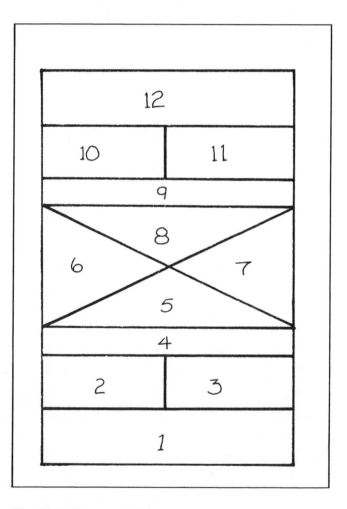

Fig. 25.3. Hopscotch Diagram.

Related Books and References

Driver's Instruction Manual. The manual from your state will include the major traffic signs used in this country.

Roucher, Nancy. "Experience an Abstract Mood." *Instructor*, vol. 97, no. 4 (November/December, 1987), p. 70.

26

MEASUREMENT

How Big Is a Foot?
Rolf Myller
New York: Atheneum, 1962

Summary

Beds had not been invented, so the king decided to have one constructed for the queen, since she had everything else. Counting paces as he walked around the queen, he estimated the bed's size to be 3' x 6'. Unfortunately, the finished product was much too small since the apprentice who made the bed had smaller feet. A mold of the king's foot produced a standard of measurement and the bed fit perfectly.

Science Topic Areas

Measurement, arbitrary units of measure

Content Related Words

Mile, yard, foot, inch, kilometer, decimeter, meter, centimeter

Activities

1. When reading the book, stop after the apprentice goes to jail and see if the children can predict the ending. Write down the predictions to see how accurate they were.

2. Cut a soda straw to the length of each child's foot so that they have their own personal standard of measurement. Estimate the size of common items such as a pencil, table top, and book, then measure them to see how accurate the predictions are. Measure a variety of objects in the classroom, library media center, or cafeteria. Try to include some large items, such as a door, window, or chalk board.

3. Have children lie on a large piece of paper and trace their outlines. Have them measure their sizes in "soda straws."

4. Divide the children into teams and have each team decide on one of the soda straws as a standard measure of length. Find objects that are the same length as the soda straws. This works well in conjunction with a nature walk.

5. Using the index finger as another unit of measurement, estimate the size of an object, then check by measuring it. Why does everyone have different answers? Is this practical in the real world? What could be done to solve this?

6. Standard units of measure such as the inch, yard, centimeter, and meter can be learned by estimating lengths of objects and then measuring them. Work in pairs and see which pair has the greatest number of correct estimates.

7. Borrow a metal measure from a shoe store and figure out the actual shoe size and width for each child. Does anyone have a copy of their footprint in a baby book? How does it compare to this measurement? What other implements can be used to measure people's sizes?

8. Display a series of objects that will fit one inside the other. Let the class guess the order in which they fit, without handling or touching the items.

9. Have the children measure their beds at home. Are they 3' x 6'? Measure other sized beds in the house. Are they smaller or larger than 3' x 6'?

10. Have children make up stories for the invention of other units, e.g., liquid measure equals how much the king drank in one day; distance is how far the king went on his daily stroll; time is the length of the king's dinner, etc. Write these down as stories and illustrate them.

11. Write a TV or radio script of the story and act it out or make paper bag characters and have a puppet show.

12. Let the children walk barefoot in brightly colored water-based paint and make a large wall mural.

13. Make abstract art pictures in which all lines are the length of the children's soda straw. Shapes and colors may vary.

14. Make a scale plan of the room and its contents using graph paper with 1-inch squares. Each square will equal 1 foot.

15. Measure common distances in your school, using standard English measurement, metric, or both. You might begin with the room measurements, the distance to the cafeteria, the size of your desk, etc.

16. How many different devices can be used to measure length? If there is an industrial arts/homemaking department in the school, check with them. What is the specific purpose of each of these tools?

17. Hang a measuring chart on the wall so students can see how tall they are now and speculate about how tall they would like to be. Explain why you would like to be the height you have chosen, e.g., to be tall enough to play basketball.

18. If the school has a mascot, ask for permission to paint big footprints of that animal on the sidewalk. Mark walkways from the exit door to the bus area, the playground, or fire drill safety spots. How big would these footprints actually be? Should they be enlarged to be more visible?

19. Stretch a rubber band around an empty milk carton from end to end. Place two pencils between the elastic and the milk carton and pluck the elastic (see figure 26.1). Move the pencils to different positions. How does length affect the pitch?

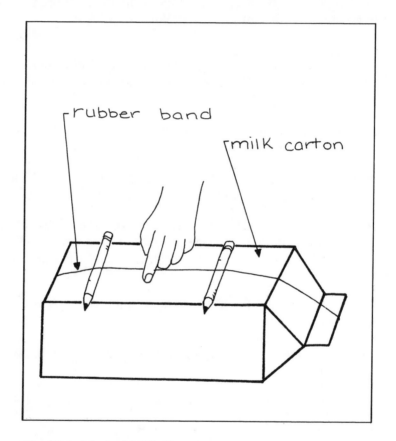

Fig. 26.1. Musical Milk Carton.

20. Look up books in the library media center on making musical instruments that demonstrate how the length of the vibrating body produces different pitches.

21. Have relay races that concentrate on using feet — hopping, jumping, skipping, three-legged races, etc. This is particularly exciting if children put on dress-up clothes over their own clothes before running to the goal and back. The dress-up clothes are removed and passed to the next person in line. This adds a problem-solving challenge to the physical feature of the race.

22. Run traditional races and events such as the broad jump. Estimate the distances before measuring them.

23. Have bean bag tosses. Estimate the length of your toss, then measure to see how close you were. Pick specific distance, such as 10 feet, and try to toss the bean bag that far. How accurate can you be?

Related Books and References

Cline, Dallas. "Making Simple Instruments for Children." *Music Educator's Journal*, vol. 66, no. 6 (February, 1980).

Johnston, Tony. *Farmer Mack Measures His Pig*. New York: Harper and Row, 1986.

27

ENERGY AND MOTION

Choo Choo
Virginia Lee Burton
Boston: Houghton Mifflin, 1937

Summary

Choo Choo, the little steam engine, was very tired of pulling a long line of passenger cars. One day she took off alone, over the hills, through the cities, and into the country where she ran out of steam. Choo Choo was rescued by the Streamliner and returned home, happy to be back with those who loved her.

Science Topic Areas

Energy conservation (heat to mechanical), simple machines, force, and momentum

Content Related Words

Speed, distance, inertia, momentum, freight, passengers

Activities

1. Choo Choo was tired of pulling heavy passenger cars. Simulate this by having relay races. Pull various weights in a wagon, e.g., a dictionary, a cement block, etc. In other races, carry weights, e.g., a bag of sugar, a brick, etc. How does the increased weight affect your efficiency? Do you get tired?

2. Tie a piece of rope onto a large piece of cardboard and pull it up a grassy or snowy slope. Slide down the hill, then pull it up again, with someone sitting on the cardboard. Is there a change? What happens when you slide down together?

3. Use a wide board or other device to make an inclined plane. Have races with identical toy trucks that have been weighted with differing amounts of stones. Predict the winners before the race. Use vehicles that are not the same shape or weight. What will happen? Add identical loads. Do the results change?

4. If you put a board in front of the moving vehicles, what happens to the vehicles and to the contents of the trucks?

5. Make two inclined planes which touch the floor opposite each other, about a yard apart. Release a toy vehicle from each side and observe which one reaches the floor first, and which one will bounce the farthest as they collide. Use toys that are not the same weight, size, or shape. Keep track of the results. Vary the angle of the ramp and see what effect this has. Do the results follow any pattern? (See figure 27.1.)

Fig. 27.1. Double Inclined Planes (Crashing Cars).

6. Set up two inclined planes or ramps to represent the open drawbridge that Choo Choo crossed. Use wind-up cars to see if it is possible to jump the gap and land on the other side. How much distance can the cars jump?

7. Make a bulletin board poster or a mural showing a side view of Choo Choo. Label the simple machines that combine to make the engine, e.g., the cow catcher is a wedge, and the train rides on a series of wheels and axles. Other examples in the book include the drawbridge, which is both a lever and an inclined plane, and the train derrick, which uses a pulley.

8. Bring in hand tools and nonelectrical kitchen utensils to see what simple machines they exemplify and how they work. Can you write this in words well enough that someone could guess the tool by the description?

9. Speed is measured in miles per hour (mph). What does this mean? Does an object need to move for a whole hour for its speed to be measured? Check your speed by measuring

how far you can run in one minute. To get mph, multiply this number by 60 (minutes in an hour) and divide by 5,280 (feet in a mile). Calculators will make this easier.

10. Check how far you can walk, skip, hop, run, jog, etc., in 1 minute. Put these on a bar graph. You can use the actual distance instead of converting to mph this time.

11. Objects usually start slowly, then go faster. This is acceleration. You can see this by poking a tiny hole in a paper cup and filling it with water. Walk along holding the cup to your side and observe the drops on the pavement. As you walk faster and faster, what happens to the distance between the drops? Vary your speed and see what happens.

12. Make a "Speed Line" comparing the speed of various animals and forms of transportation. This can become a very large display and might be an attractive addition to the library media center. Use a large ball of twine which has been knotted every 10 or 12 inches. The distance between two knots represents 10 mph. Make cards showing the name and average speed of the following:

spider—1 mph

elephant—25 mph

greyhound—40 mph

squirrel—12 mph

grizzly-bear—30 mph

cheetah—70 mph

lion—50 mph

antelope—61 mph

chicken—9 mph

Queen Mary cruise ship (1935)—35 mph

United States cruise ship (1952)—38 mph

American family car—legal speed 55 mph (or 65 mph)

These following figures represent records held by various vehicles:

Amtrak Metroliner train—98 mph

Amtrak Connecticut Yankee—83 mph

Union Pacific freight train—63 mph

France, TGV passenger train—135 mph

Japan, Yamabiko train—128 mph

airplane (piston engine)—338 mph

airplane (turboprop)—541 mph

airplane (jet engine)—988 mph

helicopter (long-distance flight) — 36 mph

1906 Stanley Steamer auto — 128 mph

Indianapolis race car — 170 mph

Daytona Beach race car — 148 mph

Additional information can be found in the *World Almanac* if you wish to add to these examples. *Note*: Ship speed was converted from knots (nautical miles).

13. When the water boils in an ordinary tea kettle, the attached whistle will produce noises. What makes this happen? How is this like Choo Choo's engine? What is burned to make the train go?

14. When water turns into steam it can produce motion. You can prove this by making popcorn. As the kernels are heated, the moisture inside the seed turns to steam, the heart of the seed gets bigger and the shell bursts. To observe the force of the popped kernels, spread a sheet on the floor and place a popcorn popper in the middle of it. Pop about ¼ cup of kernels, but do not cover the popper. Measure the distances the popped corn can travel.

15. When Choo Choo began to run out of steam (fuel) she did not stop immediately. Imitate Choo Choo's last few minutes before stopping. Describe or pantomime other objects that run out of energy or fuel, e.g., a car, a music box. How do you feel when you "run out of steam"?

16. Has anyone in the class ridden on a passenger or excursion train? What was it like?

17. Is there still a railroad going through your town? Is it a passenger train, a freight train, or are there both? Can you visit the station and observe a train arriving and departing? Is there an old station that has been remodeled for new use?

18. If there is no train, find out about the nearest passenger train from a travel agent, or call Amtrak 1-800-USA RAIL for information and a time schedule.

19. Your grandmother wants to take you on a train trip across the country. Consult the time schedule to determine your departure time and city, arrival time and city, number of stops, and services available (meals, sleeping accommodations, etc.). What are the advantages and disadvantages of train travel, compared to cars, buses, airplanes? Make a comparison chart.

20. When you are on this trip, what states will you pass through? How many miles will this be? If the train can average 60 miles an hour, how many hours will you be traveling? How many days does that equal? Make a list of items you will take with you to help pass the time or increase your enjoyment of the journey, e.g., camera, books, tape recorder with headphones, atlas, etc.

21. Dramatize the story of Choo Choo and tape record it. Sound effects will be one of the most important features of the recording.

22. Compare the book *Choo Choo* to *The Little Engine That Could*. Both trains are portrayed as though they were human beings. As a group, brainstorm the type of personality the engines are given, and how they are alike and different. What qualities or characteristics would you attribute to each of them? Write which engine you think is more admirable or which one you prefer. How does the whole class feel?

23. Numerous books and songs have been written about the history of railroads and life on the railroads. Ask your library media specialist and music teacher to help locate some of these materials, or check out the public library.

24. Is there a retired railroad worker who would be willing to talk about "the good old days" of the railroads?

25. Most anthologies of poetry have selections about railroads. Often they are compared to animate objects, e.g., horses, dragons, snakes. Write some poetry about railroad trains. Do they remind you of persons, animals, other objects? Your finished copy could be pasted on a colored cutout of a train engine or one of the cars to make a visual display.

26. Model or miniature train collecting is a popular hobby. The trains are very detailed and made to scale. Make a display of model railroad equipment for the whole school. The library media center is an excellent place for the event. Owners could show off their models and explain how they work.

27. Some areas have model railroad shows. This would be an exciting field trip if it could be arranged. Models usually cover the whole history of railroading.

Related Books and References

Jensen, Oliver. *The American Heritage History of Railroads in America*. New York: American Heritage Publishing, 1975.

Larrick, Nancy. *Piping Down the Valleys Wild: Poetry for the Young of All Ages*. New York: Delacorte Press, 1985.

Piper, Watty. *The Little Engine That Could*. New York: Platt and Munk, 1961.

Songs and Sounds of the Great Days of Steam. New York: American Heritage Publishing, 1975. (A sound recording)

28

BUOYANCY

Who Sank the Boat?

Pamela Allen
New York: Coward-McCann, 1982

Summary

This rhyming fantasy tells the tale of a cow, a donkey, a sheep, a pig, and a mouse who attempt to go for a boat ride but end up in the water instead. The problem remains to find out who really sank the boat.

Science Topic Areas

Buoyancy, balance, characteristics of matter—size, weight

Content Related Words

Buoyancy, capsize, float, balance, bay

Activities

1. Design and make an aluminum foil boat that will both float and carry a load. How many paper clips does it take to sink each boat? Which shaped boat holds the most paper clips, and which holds the fewest? Children should record their observations using descriptive sentences, pictures, or charts. (Use a piece of foil 1" x 2" to make the boat. Small trays or plastic cartons will hold liquid to simulate the water in the bay.)

2. Repeat this experiment using small uniform-sized objects as boats. The individual serving-size containers restaurants use for butter, jelly, and coffee cream are ideal for

this purpose. Have children estimate how many paper clips (or other objects) will be needed to sink the container. Do the "boats" sink simultaneously if the same number of paper clips is added?

3. Use coins (pennies, nickels, dimes, and quarters) to show how boats can be balanced to stay afloat. Distribute the coins evenly in one small plastic cup but stack them to one side in another cup. What is the result? Can the pile be rearranged so the cup stays afloat?

4. Use several sizes of coins to sink a small plastic cup. Which order of placement allows the greatest number of objects to be placed in the boat?

5. The book says that Mr. Peffer lived beside a sea. Try the same experiment using water with several spoons of salt dissolved into it.

6. Guess the number of objects that will fit into a given space using any uniform set of objects, such as marbles or macaroni. The reverse of this is to guess how many items are in a jar, e.g., dried peas, jelly beans.

7. Estimate the size or volume of objects. Waterproof, sinking objects such as marbles or pebbles can be measured by placing them into a glass container of water (see figure 28.1). The difference in the water level of the cup is the volume of the object. Specific measurements can be made or general comparisons can be observed.

8. Select several items and have the children predict if they will sink or float in a dishpan of water, e.g., a cork, a styrofoam ball, a golf ball, a bottle cap, a coin, etc. Use different forms of the same material and see if the result is the same, e.g., a block of wood, a popsicle stick, a pencil. Chart your results.

9. What happens to an ice cube which is put into a cup of water? Put the ice cube into a cup of water that has salt dissolved in it and compare the results. What does this tell you about the ocean or bodies of water like the Great Salt Lake? Use a larger chunk of ice and put it into a pan of fresh water and then salt water. Are the results the same as with the ice cube?

10. The body of water in the book is a bay. What is a bay? If your state has a coastline, locate the bays nearest you. If you are inland, pick another section of the country or look on a globe for bays.

11. The animals were not aware of boating safety rules. Make up a list of rules you should follow if you are boating or canoeing. Is there a local boating club that could provide a set of regulations to compare with yours?

12. If you have a swimming pool available, practice capsizing a boat and learning to right it. What safety rules pertain when there has been a boating mishap, e.g., don't leave the boat and try to swim to shore.

Fig. 28.1. Displacement of Water Experiment.

13. Life preservers should be worn in boats at all times. A catalog from the sporting goods store or a discount house would show various kinds and sizes. What size would each child need to wear? What would the teacher need? Bring in life preservers and demonstrate how they must be worn.

14. Find in the library media center some safe water rules to observe while swimming. There are a variety of references, including government publications and recreational association magazines. Is there a pool in your town where you can take swimming lessons? Can you take a lifesaving course?

15. Suppose Mr. Peffer keeps a diary. Write an entry for the day of this fateful trip? What emotions do you think he had? Was it humorous? Was he angry?

16. Read *Mr. Gumpy's Outing*, which is very similar to *Who Sank the Boat?* Choose someone to role play Mr. Gumpy and Mr. Peffer. Have them discuss their feelings about the experience they each had. How do they feel about another boat ride?

17. Write a sequel to this story telling what happens if Mr. Peffer decides to invite his friends for another ride. Illustrate your story.

18. Get sporting goods catalogs from local or mail order stores. What type boat would be most appropriate for this group of animals? Should it have sails or a motor? Compare prices of similar boats.

19. A dory is a small fishing boat that resembles Mr. Peffer's boat. Make a dory mobile using the pattern in figure 28.2. Use two sticks or twigs and attach several boats to each one. Then connect both of these sticks to a main stick. When they are tied together, the boats should all be balanced.

20. "Row, Row, Row Your Boat" is a very well-known singing round. Try putting new words with the melody to tell the story of the animals' boat trip. "Sailing, Sailing Over the Bounding Main" is another possibility.

21. Cruises are popular vacation choices. Ask a travel agent for folders from several cruise lines. What do these ships offer for recreation and entertainment? Note the cutaway diagram of the various decks on the ship. How would a boat like this suit Mr. Peffer and his friends?

Related Books and References

Burningham, John. *Mr. Gumpy's Outing*. Holt, Rinehart and Winston, 1970.

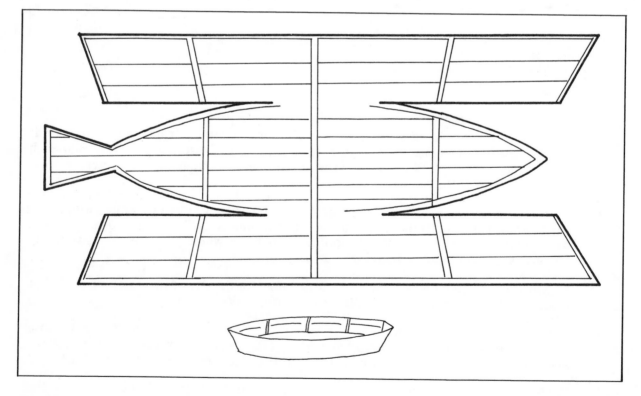

Fig. 28.2. Making a Dory Model.

29

FORCE AND MOVEMENT

Mr. Gumpy's Motorcar

John Burningham
New York: Thomas Crowell, 1973

Summary

An automobile ride turns into a muddy experience when a sudden shower catches Mr. Gumpy and his friends in the middle of the fields. Unfortunately, no one wants to be the one to help get the car unstuck, but the animals learn that cooperation helps them solve the problem.

Science Topic Areas

Movement, push, pull, work

Content Related Words

Force, friction, acceleration, momentum

Activities

1. This story does not take place in the United States. Using the text and illustrations, can you figure out where the author lives? Where is this country and in what direction would you go to visit him? Could you go there in an automobile?

2. If you had been in Mr. Gumpy's car, what other solutions might you have offered for getting the car free, e.g., gravel under the wheels. Make this a convincing and possible alternative.

3. Mr. Gumpy and his friends were very dirty when they returned. If you had been one of them, how would you have explained why the car got stuck in the mud? What did they have to do to free it from the mud? Why did this work?

4. Make a labeled, bulletin board display showing pictures of antique, classic, and present-day cars. Put them in order by the year they were made. How have automobiles changed since Mr. Gumpy's car was made?

5. Does anyone you know have an antique or classic car that the class could see? What are some advantages and disadvantages of owning such a car?

6. What types of vehicles can you buy if you must travel on muddy or unimproved roads, in the snow, in desert areas?

7. Make a survey of the different types of cars and trucks owned by parents or teachers. How many vehicles does each family own? Which models are most popular? Categorize these by kind, manufacturer, use.

8. You are a used-car salesman trying to convince a buyer that this car will not become easily stuck in the mud. What arguments will you use? (Be truthful!) What tips can you give the buyer on driving under difficult conditions? (See a driver's manual of rules for suggestions.)

9. Design a car of the future. What shape is probably best? Will the car of the future have different purposes, fuel source, capacity, artistic qualities, comfort features?

10. Bring a child's wagon to class and experiment with pulling it over various "roads" to see the effect on the "passengers" (a dishpan of water on a towel or a pile of books would serve the purpose). Pull the wagon over a carpeted floor, a slippery wood or linoleum floor, grass, a sidewalk, a gravel driveway, and "rumble strips" made of a layer of rulers, pencils, etc. Rank which trip is easiest for the person pulling the wagon, and for the "passenger"? Try lighter and heavier objects to compare how much effort you must use.

11. Predict the results of an experiment in which objects are moved in a wagon, e.g., will it be easier to move one child up a hill or two children on flat ground, one larger child or two small children, one tall, thin child or one short, solid child? For each set of children, push the wagon, then pull it. Which way requires less effort?

12. Put an object on an inclined plane and attach a rope to the object. Bring the rope over the top of the incline, attach a can or pail to it, and gradually add weights to the can (see figure 29.1). How much weight does it take to move the object? Change the surface by covering it with waxed paper, foil, or sandpaper and compare the amount of weight needed. Attach objects of differing size to the rope and compare how many weights must be used to move it.

13. Have races using toy cars and a small inclined plane track. How can cars be made to go faster? How can the surface be prepared to increase the speed of the cars?

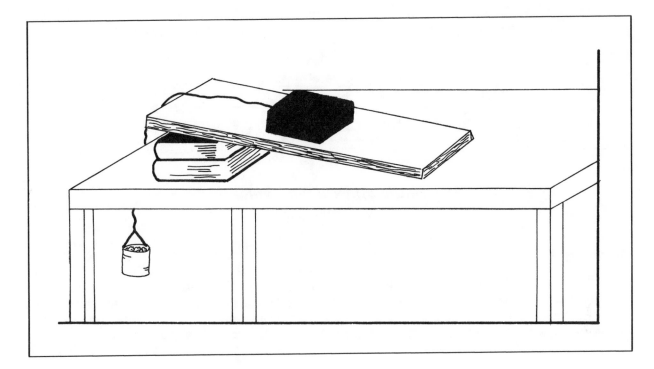

Fig. 29.1. Objects Moving on an Inclined Plane.

14. Help rearrange the classroom desks and furniture. Is it easier to push the furniture, pull it, or have two people carry it?

15. Have the class cooperate in deciding how they could use the knowledge of machines to move a large number of books in the library media center.

16. Have tug-of-war contests. Set up different groups of people to see if some have an advantage, e.g., tall students vs. short students. Also have each group stand on a different surface (grass vs. pavement, carpet vs. smooth floor) to see if it gives an advantage to one team. Can you explain the results?

17. Many popular songs have been written over the years about cars. Can you find old ones like "In My Merry Oldsmobile," or more modern ones such as "409" and "Little Deuce Coupe" by the Beach Boys?

Related Books and References

Best of the Beach Boys. 2 vols. Capitol recording.

Birnie, W. A. H., ed. *Reader's Digest Family Songbook*. Pleasantville, N.Y.: Reader's Digest Association, 1977.

Burton, Virginia. *Choo Choo*. Boston: Houghton Mifflin, 1987.

Cole, Joanna. *Cars and How They Go*. New York: Thomas Crowell, 1983.

30

WEATHER, SEASONS, AND STATES OF MATTER

Sadie and the Snowman

Allen Morgan
New York: Scholastic, 1985

Summary

Sadie loves to build snowmen, even though they always melt. She knows she can build another one the next time it snows. As the days grow warmer, Sadie realizes this is the last snowman of the year and tries to protect it from the warming sun. Soon only a pan of water remains. She freezes the liquid in a plastic bag and next year's first snowman is already started.

Science Topic Areas

States of matter, weather, seasons of the year, animal tracks

Content Related Words

Melt, freeze

Activities

1. After a snowfall, walk around the school yard and find the places where the amount of snow is the greatest and the smallest. Make a chart indicating the locations and amount of snow. Predict reasons for the variation in depth. Remeasure these same places in a few days to see if there is more or less snow. What has happened to produce different measurements? Chart these numbers and compare them to the original figures.

2. Patterns of light and shadow will appear on the snowy school yard. Sunny areas will be heated and the snow will melt sooner. Map the areas of sun and shadow and use

thermometers to check the actual temperature of the areas. Repeat this at another time of the day. Do the shadows remain in the same place? Is the temperature difference consistent?

3. Wind moves snow around at the school yard and forms little snow dunes. How do fences, walls, and other standing objects affect the formation of these dunes?

4. Icicles form at the edge of the roof as the sun turns snow to water and back to ice. Are icicles always on the same side of the building? Does their length differ in various spots?

5. As the snow is falling, catch flakes on pieces of dark construction paper. Quickly observe them with a hand lens or magnifying glass. Notice the patterns that are formed. A glass of snow will melt inside the classroom, but the container will no longer be full. Place similar glasses of snow in various parts of the classroom, e.g., next to the windows, near a heat source, in a dark closet, etc. Which container of snow melts first, last? Why? What has the melted snow become? What happens if this liquid is heated in a tea kettle?

6. The drawing in figure 30.1 shows the tracks of three common animals. Compare each animal's front paws to its hind print. The smaller figures represent a short trail made by each animal. The position of the prints represents the way in which the animal moves. Which animal is fastest, slowest, drags its tail? Compare the three sets of tracks to make hypotheses and observations about these animals. Make a print of your own hand or foot. Compare its size and shape to those of the animals. What are the most distinguishing characteristics of human prints?

7. Make sets of tracks on index cards—one animal per card. Have children try to guess the animal before checking in a resource book. Match the tracks to magazine pictures of the animal for a display.

8. Using the identification cards as a guide, draw track scenarios, e.g., an animal hopping then running, one animal being pursued by another, etc. Can others guess what event is occurring?

9. Tracks made by humans and animals are easier to follow in wet sand or after a snowfall. Locate and study some animal tracks and write what you think the animal is doing, based on the visual evidence. Do the same for tracks made by children. (Birdseed left on the ground overnight should attract animals and birds so there will be tracks to study.)

10. Draw a foot track on half a raw potato. Carefully cut away the excess potato until the track protrudes about ¼ inch. Wipe this dry, then ink it. You have your own personal track stamp for making stationery, wrapping paper, etc.

11. Take a walk on a snowy day and have the children list words to describe the many characteristics of snow. Use these words to help write simple poetry such as a "Five Liner":

Fig. 30.1. Wild Animal Tracks.

Line 1—Write down a noun such as "snow."

Line 2—Write two adjectives that describe the noun.

Line 3—Write three verbs (using a participle form: -ing or -ed) telling what line 1 does.

Line 4—Write a thought about the noun using a short phrase.

Line 5—Repeat line 1 or use a synonym for that word.

Icicle

Sharp, cold

Dripping, growing, melting

Hanging stick of ice

Hard water

All words, except those in the phrase, should be separated by commas. With very young children, avoid grammatical terms and substitute "describing words" and "action words" to elicit a response. (This should be done as a group activity until children are comfortable with it.)

12. Have children write or tape stories about an experience they have had in the snow. Work on good beginnings and endings, details, and proper sequencing of events. You might begin by reading from *On the Banks of Plum Creek* by Laura Ingalls Wilder in which Pa becomes lost in the snow on the way home from town and survives by eating Christmas candy.

13. Collect pictures of winter scenes from calendars, cards, or magazines and write captions or poems to accompany them. Make a display of these in the room, hall, or library media center.

14. Divide the class into small groups and have a "snowman-snowlady" building contest. Which is the most creative sculpture? Which one lasts the longest? Which one melts first? Why did this happen?

15. Use Hans Christian Andersen's folk story "The Snow Queen" as a scenario for a video play which is planned, produced, and performed by the class.

16. Songs about snow are quite easy to find, especially in books about winter holidays from the library media center. Children are probably familiar with several, e.g., "Winter Wonderland," "Let it Snow," "Frosty the Snowman," etc.

17. If a child were going to live in a snowy climate for the first time, he or she would need heavier clothing. What essential items would that include? Look in a department store or sporting goods catalog to find styles and costs. Do some comparison shopping among items to ensure that your selection is practical and affordable.

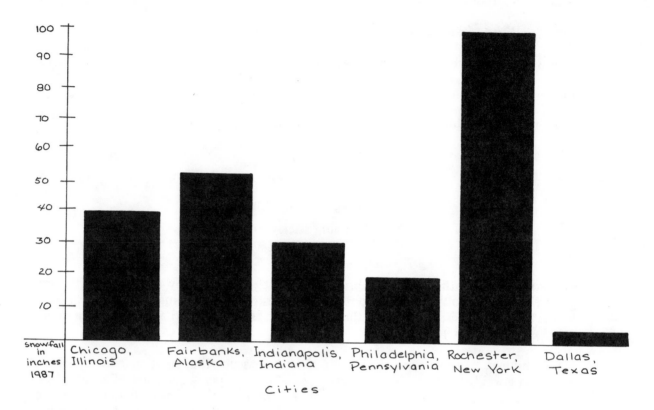

Fig. 30.2. Snowfall Comparison—Selected U.S. Cities.

18. Answer these questions by reading the graph on snowfall in figure 30.2.

   (a) Sadie could make lots of snowmen if she lived in this city.

   (b) Sadie would probably never be able to make a snowman if she lived here.

   (c) Which cities had more than 30 inches of snow in 1987?

   (d) Was there more snow in Indianapolis or in Philadelphia?

   (e) Alaska is the most northern state in the United States. Does that mean that Fairbanks is always the snowiest city?

   (f) What does this graph tell you about snowfall in 1986?

Note: The drifting and tracking activities of this unit can be simulated using sand or sandy soil.

Related Books and References

Burton, Virginia Lee. *Katy and the Big Snow*. Boston: Houghton Mifflin, 1943.

Keats, Ezra Jack. *The Snowy Day*. New York: Viking Press, 1962.

Murie, Olaus. *A Field Guide to Animal Tracks*. Boston: Houghton Mifflin, 1975.

Wilder, Laura Ingalls. *On the Banks of Plum Creek*. New York: Harper and Row, 1971.

31

CHEMICAL AND PHYSICAL CHANGE

Strega Nona's Magic Lessons
Tomie dePaola
New York: Harcourt Brace Jovanovich, 1982

Summary

Bambolona is tired of working for her father, the baker, and sets off to learn magic from Strega Nona. Big Anthony is hired to replace her, but jealously tries to learn witchcraft, too. His efforts at baking and magic both meet with disastrous results.

Science Topic Areas

Chemical change, physical change

Content Related Words

Yeast, dough, "grazie," "sì signore," "mamma mia," "strega"

Note: Chemical changes are usually indicated by the production of a gas, a new smell, the clouding of a solution, fire, or a change in color. In a physical change, the original object remains intact or can be retrieved, despite a change in appearance.

Activities

1. Following directions on the package, grow yeast. This is best done in a glass or clear plastic container, so that the height of the yeast can be measured. Make comparisons such as these:

- dry yeast vs. cake yeast

- yeast (either kind) with 1 tablespoon of sugar added

- yeast (either kind) with 2 tablespoons of sugar added

- yeast that is outdated

- yeast that is outdated but has sugar added

Record your observations and measurements in a notebook, using sketches and word descriptions. Do this for all the experiments in this unit. Label the materials and equipment used and indicate the end result that is produced.

2. Water used to dissolve yeast (and water) should be about 100 degrees F. Use cold water with one package and hot water with another. What happens? Why is this so?

3. Let some of the yeast "work" in a glass container that can be stoppered. Put one end of a piece of plastic tubing through the stopper and put the other end into bromothymol blue solution. (See figure 31.1.) Observe the difference in the solution. Use another container of bromothymol blue and have someone breathe into it through a straw. Compare the two. (The yeast gas and the person's breath are both carbon dioxide and cause the solution to turn yellow.)

Fig. 31.1. Presence of Carbon Dioxide in Yeast Bubbles.

4. Make Bambolona's Italian bread:

    1 tablespoon of butter

    2 cups flour

    2 packages yeast

    1 tablespoon sugar

    To these ingredients add 1¾ cups hot water and beat with a mixer for 2 minutes. Add ½ cup flour and beat 2 more minutes. Add ⅔ cups flour and mix by hand until a large ball is formed. Knead for 10 minutes on a floured board. Break into 2 pieces. Flatten each one, roll it up and tuck the ends under. Place on a cornmeal-covered cookie sheet and let rise in refrigerator for 2 to 24 hours or at room temperature for ½ hour. Bake at 425 degrees F for 20 minutes. Glaze with a mixture of 1 egg white and 1 tablespoon water. Bake 5 more minutes.

5. Look at recipes for cakes and cookies in your library media center. They do not contain yeast but still rise. Which of the ingredients causes this to happen?

6. Show that baking soda can produce a gas and make things rise. Take a large balloon that is easy to inflate and put 1 tablespoon of baking soda into it. Put 3 tablespoons of vinegar into a glass soda bottle. Slip the balloon end over the bottle top and shake the soda down into the vinegar. (See figure 31.2.) Observe what happens. This also is carbon dioxide being formed. Re-create the experiment putting yeast and sugar into the balloon and water into the soda bottle.

7. Spread several drops of vinegar on the copper bottom of an ordinary cooking pan. Sprinkle table salt onto the vinegar and wipe it around with your fingers. What happens? Add more vinegar and salt as needed. (A very dilute acidic solution is formed chemically and cleans the dirt from the copper.)

8. In a well-ventilated room, clean the bottom of a copper pan or a piece of sterling silver with household ammonia. What do you observe? (The ammonia actually unites with the copper or silver to clean off the oxide which had formed.) Are these chemical or physical changes?

9. Big Anthony tried to turn the iron pot into gold. For many centuries, people called alchemists attempted to do this. Use the card catalog in the library media center to look up stories of the alchemists. Are there fairy tales of other legends of people who tried to turn ordinary items into gold?

10. When Big Anthony disguised himself, it was only a physical change. An object can look very different but still be the same. For example, put a tray of water into the freezer. How does it change? Leave the tray at room temperature. Will the result be like the original? This can be repeated, but the change will always be physical.

11. Objects can combine to look very different yet remain the same. Mix a spoon of salt and a spoon of pepper together. Describe the result. Run a comb through your hair or

Fig. 31.2. Household Products Produce Gas to Inflate Balloon.

brush it against some wool. Hold the comb close to the mixture. What happens? (The pepper will separate from the salt and adhere to the comb. The change is physical.)

12. Strega Nona must heat her potions to make them work. Fire is another chemical change. Light a candle and watch it burn. What are all the chemical changes you can observe (odor, smoke, color change, heat, charring of wick)?

13. The story takes place in Calabria. Locate this region on a map of Italy.

14. Perhaps Bambolona sang as she worked. Sing some Italian folk songs or listen to a sample of Italian music (orchestral, operatic, etc.). Records or tapes may be available in your library media center.

15. Bambolona gets up to work before the sun rises. What time of day would this be where you live? Is it the same all year? When would her shortest work days be if she works from dawn until dusk? When are the longest?

16. Have a dress-up day and try to fool everyone as Big Anthony did.

17. If you wanted to show Strega Nona that you had magic powers, what would you do? Write this out, indicating what you wish to achieve, how you would do it, and what the results will be.

18. Visit a bakery to see bread being made. Pizza parlors also use yeast dough for crust and may invite you for a visit (and a sample). Write a language experience story about the trip.

19. How many different kinds of bread, e.g., wheat, rye, pumpernickel, does your supermarket sell? How many companies sell their products there? Compare the cost of 1 pound of bread of various kinds and various companies. What is the difference in price between a 1-pound loaf of white bread bought in the supermaket and one purchased at a bakery?

20. Leave one slice each of commercial and bakery bread out in the air. Observe what changes take place. Put a slice of each in a closed plastic bag for several days. What happens? Which activity represents a physical change in the bread? Which one indicates a chemical change?

21. Design a wedding cake like Bambolona had to make. Use drawing materials, colored construction paper, foil paper, etc.

22. Make Strega Nona dolls or hanging ornaments from dried apples, cornhusks, or even bread dough. Books on dollmaking from the library media center can provide many helpful ideas. Paint or decorate them with scraps of cloth and felt.

23. Make bread dough for Strega Nona doll ornaments:

4 cups flour

1 cup salt

1½ cups water

Combine salt and flour in large bowl. Add water and mix well by hand. Knead this on a floured board until smooth and elastic. Break off balls and form into shapes. Moisten pieces to make them adhere to each other and place dolls on a cookie sheet. Bake at 300 degrees F about 10 minutes or until lightly browned. Cool and dry completely before painting with tempera or acrylics. Spray varnish for a shiny finish. A paper clip can be molded onto the back of the head before baking so that a hook can be attached for hanging.

Related Books and References

Pavarotti, Luciano. *Neapolitan Songs*. London recording.

Steig, William. *Solomon, the Rusty Nail*. New York: Farrar, Straus and Giroux, 1985.

32

BALLOONS AND GASES

The Big Balloon Race

Eleanor Coerr
New York: Harper and Row, 1981

Summary

Carlotta the Great had just lifted off for a very important balloon race when she discovered her daughter Ariel was a stowaway. Despite the problems of extra weight, however, the women win the race—with a little ingenius assistance from Ariel.

Science Topic Areas

Balloons, buoyancy, lighter-than-air gases, heating and cooling of air, winds, directions

Content Related Words

Aeronaut (astronaut), hydrogen, crosswing, ballast, updraft, ripcord, toggles, altimeter, compass, valve

Activities

1. Get several regular round balloons. Let children blow up some of them and tie them. Have the remaining balloons filled with helium and tied shut. Let them loose in the classroom. What happens? Why?

2. Attach a small cup to the string on each helium balloon and fill it with weights (paper clips, coins) until it maintains a stable place in midair. Choose a starting and finish line and have a race. If this is done in the classroom, a fan may be needed to provide air currents. Why did that particular balloon win?

3. Simple ways can be used to tell wind direction. Tack a piece of ribbon or plastic surveyor's tape about a yard long on top of a pole stuck in the ground. A hanging windsock can be made by cutting the leg off an old pair of pants. Secure an embroidery hoop around the larger opening. Hang this so that it is free to move and catch the wind.

4. Check the air currents around your school or even in the classroom by making a pinwheel (figure 32.1) and seeing where it spins the most. You might try to count the number of revolutions it makes while someone is timing it with a stopwatch. How many times did it spin in one minute? Was the speed constant? What places have the strongest air currents?

Fig. 32.1. The Pinwheel.

5. Does warm or cool air rise? Measure the temperature of your classroom on the floor, at about waist level, just above your ear, and near the ceiling. Make a bar graph of the temperatures starting with the coolest (blue), and going in order to the highest (use green, yellow, then red). These color bands represent a thermograph such as in infrared photography. They are also used on colored newspaper weather maps to show ranges of temperature.

6. Tie cards with the class name and address to some of the helium balloons and set them free. How far do they travel? What happens to the balloons you leave in the classroom? On your card be sure to include the name, full address, and telephone number of the school, your grade and teacher, and the date of the launching. It is important to explain very briefly what your project is, and how you would like the finder of the balloon to contact you.

7. From what you have observed about wind direction near your school, which way do you predict the balloons will go? Looking at a map of your town, what will they pass over on their flight? What direction is this?

8. Locate a detailed county or regional highway map in the library media center and post it in the classroom so that pins can be used to mark the spots where balloons were retrieved. Record the distance and number of days each balloon traveled. These figures can be used to figure statistics such as number of miles covered each day. Do all the balloons travel in the same direction?

9. Participate in a national balloon launch. For information write to the National Science Teachers Association, 1742 Connecticut Avenue, NW, Washington D.C. 20009.

10. On a map locate the key or compass rose. How do they show which direction indicates north, south, east, west? Does north always point the same way on every map?

11. Learn to read a compass. Set the compass in an open space such as the playground and list the places you see at each of the major compass points. In which direction is your home, the sports field, the downtown business district, etc.?

12. Balloonists take trips of several days today. Make a list of items you would take—both essential and "luxury" ones. In an emergency, which kinds of goods would you toss overboard first?

13. A local TV station is giving away balloon rides as part of an advertising campaign. To win, you must write an essay explaining why you want to take a balloon ride. You must convince them in about 150 words.

14. Your rich uncle has just bought a hot air balloon. He has volunteered to answer all the questions your classmates have, then give them a tethered ride. Make a list of all the things you would like to know about balloons—size, material, cost, where it was purchased, etc.

15. Have the class make a life-size outline of a modern balloon on the playground or gym floor. Mark the outline with chalk. How many steps is it from top to bottom and from side to side? How many people fit in the basket for a trip?

16. There are many new or unique words in the book. Make a list and then scramble the letters. Exchange them with a friend and see who can figure them out first.

17. Consult the library media center to find out how and why passenger pigeons were used at the time of the story. Why did Carlotta take one on her flight? What would the modern day balloonist use instead of Harry?

18. Carlotta flew 2,000 feet above the earth. What portion of a mile is this? Measure this distance straight from your school door. How many students need to stand with their arms outstretched to cover that distance? How high do modern balloons fly?

19. Listen to the type of music that may have been playing during the festivities at Carlotta's balloon launching. John Philip Sousa, "the March King," was composing band music at that time, while Stephen Foster was probably the best-known song writer of the day. Ask the library media specialist for information on these famous composers.

20. Carlotta was a real person who lived from 1849 to 1932. How old was she at the time of the race? How many years ago did this event happen?

21. Ariel also became a famous balloonist. If she asked you to help her write a book about her life, what title would you suggest? The paper jacket of a book usually contains a summary of the work or tells some incident in the book. Write this summary or incident for the cover of Ariel's book.

22. Look in a book of costumes from the library media center to see what people wore in the 1880s. Make sketches or paper dolls to show more details. How were children dressed? What hairstyles were popular?

23. The story takes place along the Mohawk River in New York state. Locate this area. What mountains lie on either side of the river? Would this have an effect on ballooning?

24. Learn more about hot air balloon races from magazines, or write for information: Albuquerque International Balloon Fiesta, 4804 Hawkins St. N.E., Albuquerque, N.M., 87109.

25. Design and name your own balloon using construction paper, paints, or any media you choose. These can be placed at various heights on a large mural to simulate the race.

26. A three-dimensional balloon can also be made from paper. Cut out and assemble the basket and holder shown in figure 32.2 by pushing the tabs through the slots and taping them securely. Blow up and tie the balloon. Measure the distance from the basket rim, through the holder, around the top of the balloon and back to the basket rim. Cut several pieces of string this length and soak them in dilute school glue. Wrap the strings over the balloon and attach to the basket. Let dry and suspend your creation.

27. Celebrate the end of your project with a "balloon cake." Two 8- or 9-inch cake layers are placed about 6 inches apart on a foil-covered cardboard. The bottom piece is cut straight across the top, about two inches down, to form the top of the basket. Colored frostings can be used to make stripes or other designs, or use cake sprinkles and small candies to achieve the effect. Shoestring licorice forms the strings that hold the balloon to the basket. Enjoy!

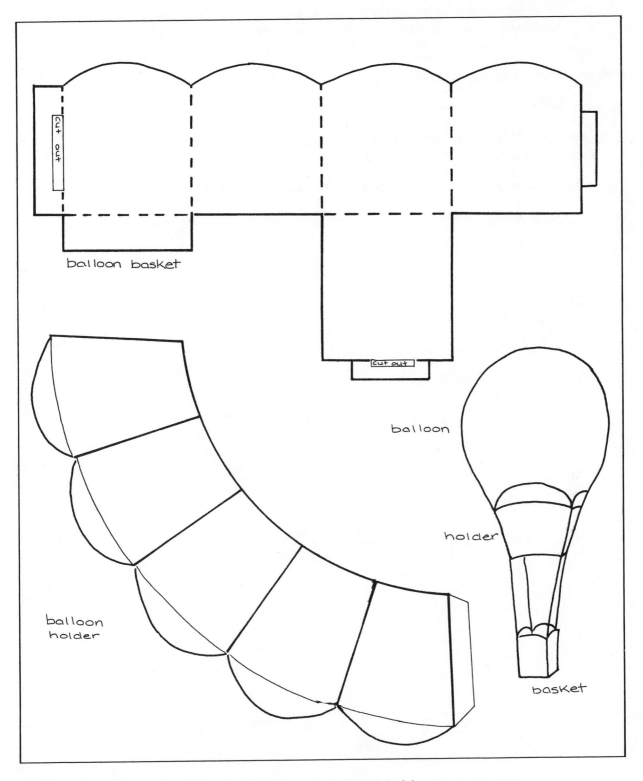

balloon basket

cut out

balloon

holder

balloon holder

basket

Fig. 32.2. Pattern for a Three-Dimensional Hot Air Balloon Model.

28. Some schools have a parachute for use in physical education classes. Activities with the parachute would help children visualize some of the concepts of the book.

Related Books and References

Calhoun, Mary. *Hot Air Henry*. New York: Morrow, 1981.

Hillerman, Tony. "A Ballooning Interest: Albuquerque's Hot-Air Festival." *National Geographic Traveler*, vol. 2, no. 2 (summer 1985), pp. 142-149.

Lamorisse, Albert. *The Red Balloon*. New York: Doubleday, 1956.

Worrell, Estelle Ansley. *The Doll Book*. New York: Van Nostrand Reinhold, 1966.

33

AIRPLANES

The Glorious Flight

Alice Provensen and Martin Provensen
New York: Viking Penguin, 1983

Summary

Louis Blériot had already been a successful inventor in the automobile industry, but the desire to fly became the driving force in his life. Despite numerous setbacks, he continued perfecting a machine until he became the first man to fly across the English Channel.

Science Topic Areas

History of airplane flight, lighter-than-air craft, heavier-than-air craft

Content Related Words

Airship, glider, aeronaut, motor, propellor, flying machine, café

Activities

1. Take the part of one of the members of the Blériot family and write a short article for a popular magazine of the time answering one of the following questions: Father, why do you want to fly so badly? Mother, do you approve of your husband's flying or do you feel it is too dangerous? Children, how do you feel when your friends tease you about your father and his inventions?

2. On a European map, locate Cambrai, France; Dover, England; and the English Channel. Over what body of water did Blériot fly and in which direction did he first go? The advertisement indicated "no intermediate landings." Was this possible?

3. The prize money was a thousand pounds. How much does this equal in U.S. money today? Would it be worth more or less in 1909?

4. How many years ago did Blériot start his project? How long did he work on his experimental aircrafts before this flight?

5. Blériot left France at 4:35 A.M. How long was the total journey? What time did he land in England? How many minutes did it take to fly one mile? Why did the flight have to occur between sunrise and sunset?

6. Write a newspaper story announcing Blériot's achievement. Be sure your headline will grab people's attention, and remember to include the most important details in the first paragraph—who? what? when? where? why? how? How would an English paper report the event? How would a French newspaper tell of the same happening? It might be interesting to see newspapers from other countries. Ask your library media specialist to obtain current papers from England and France.

7. Organize a paper airplane flying contest. Each participant should complete an entry form to indicate the category of entry, design and make a paper airplane (for example, see figure 33.1), participate in flying his or her plane. The class should decide the categories for judging, e.g., time aloft, distance covered, aerobatic display, aesthetic design. Must all planes stay in the air a specific amount of time? Will there be a single try or perhaps two out of three tries? Will there be a production code, i.e., no glue or tape allowed, no weights attached, etc.? Who will be allowed to enter—students? teachers? parents? classmates from other rooms? Select judges to measure distance and time flights to evaluate creativity.

8. Class members should be responsible for choosing the prizes that will be awarded in each category. These may be simple silhouettes of airplanes cut from colored paper, ribbons, certificates, etc.; or more elaborate choices may be made.

9. An excellent guide to paper airplanes called *Whitewings* can be purchased from the National Air and Space Museum, Smithsonian Institution, Dept. 0006, Washington, D.C. 20073 (price about $15.00).

10. Make a display of airplanes and rockets of various eras. These could be magazine photos or models. Sequence them from the oldest to present-day ones.

11. Look up other early aviators, including women aviation pioneers such as Amelia Earhart, Beryl Markham, Jacqueline Cochran, and Sally Ride.

12. Make models of planes from wooden or plastic building toys. Can you construct them so the wheels and propellor are movable?

13. Pilots must be knowledgeable about wind currents. Look these up in an encyclopedia or other reference book. On a large map, from the library media center, locate the major wind currents that affect the United States and the direction from which they come. How does this affect aviation? How would Blériot have been affected?

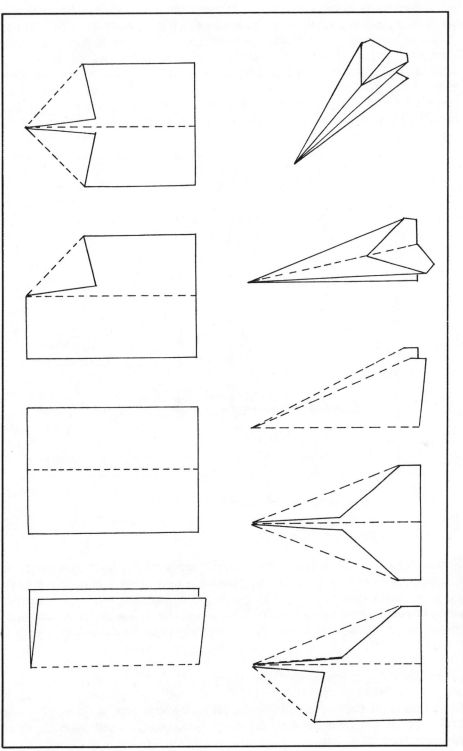

Fig. 33.1. Paper Airplane Pattern.

14. Airplanes fly because a vacuum is created against the wing. Show this with a piece of paper. (a) Hold a strip of writing paper (2" x 6") between your fingers and blow against it. What happens to the paper? (b) Hold a sheet of writing paper against the palm of your hand, which should be parallel to the floor. Blow against the paper and observe in what direction it goes. (c) Put a thumbtack in the center of a playing card and hold it beneath the hole in a thread spool (see figure 33.2). Blow into the hole at the top of the spool and let go of the playing card. What happens when you stop blowing into the spool? (These are examples of Bernoulli's principle.)

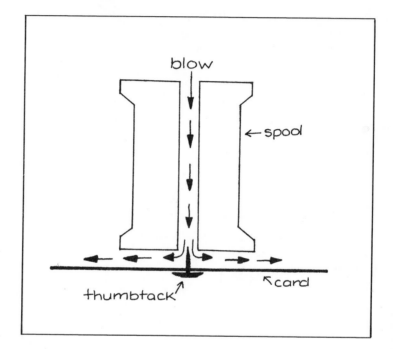

Fig. 33.2. Bernoulli's Principle.

15. Which objects move easiest in the wind? Slide several 1-inch lengths of soda straw onto a length of heavy twine. Tie the twine between two stable objects. Attach several different items (paper clip, paper plate, plant leaf, etc.) to each length of soda straw, using masking tape. Let the items "fly" along the string one at a time and observe how they move. Which ones move the fastest? This can be done inside with a small fan to provide the wind.

16. Make and fly wooden gliders (see figure 33.3). Materials needed for one glider are (a) one sheet of balsa or ash wood—1/32" x 3" x 24", (b) one piece of wood—¼" x 16", (c) 12-15 inches of thin wire, (d) sharp cutting implements, a ruler, and wood glue. You may wish to experiment with different wing shapes and sizes to increase distance covered, time aloft, etc.

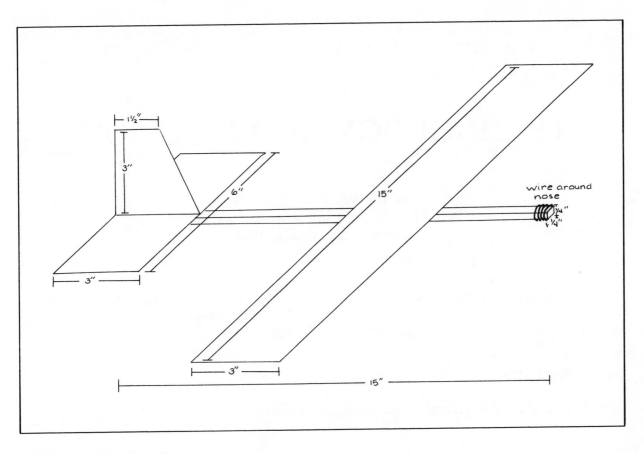

Fig. 33.3. A Wooden Glider.

Related Books and References

Sabin, Louis. *Wilbur and Orville Wright: The Flight to Adventure.* Mahwah, N.J.: Troll Associates, 1983.

34

TECHNOLOGY AND ILLUSION

The Bionic Bunny Show
Marc Brown and Laurene Krasny Brown
Boston: Little, Brown, 1984

Summary

Through the use of costumes, makeup, sets and special effects, television transforms an ordinary rabbit into a bionic superhero. The "play within a play" format allows a behind-the-scenes look at the world of illusion, as well as a glimpse at the rabbit's real life.

Science Topic Areas

Technology and illusion, television, sound, lights, bionics

Content Related Words

Bionic, microphone, cast, control room, costume, director, properties, sets, director

Activities

1. As a class, write, produce, and videotape a further episode of "The Bionic Bunny Show." To do this, you will need to select script writers, performers, a director, and persons to be in charge of costumes, properties, sets, special effects, makeup, and filming. (Teachers or parents may be needed to fill the more technical roles.) After the script is prepared, this project would probably take six to eight weeks for rehearsals and the videotaping. Before you start there are other activities that will increase your knowledge of science and other areas, and will help with your production.

2. Listen to tapes or records of old radio shows. How did they create the illusions and sound effects to aid listeners' enjoyment of the show. Watch old videos of the earliest TV shows—preferably live performances. What effects were possible? How were they limited in what they could do? Compare both of these to modern TV and the effects achieved now? (Videotape an "action" program to view in class so there is a common program to discuss.)

3. If possible visit a TV studio to see a program in production or watch one of the TV shows that have been made to show how special-effects movies are filmed, e.g., *Star Wars*, or *Superman*.

4. If there is an auditorium in your school or in a nearby building, have the teacher arrange a tour of the backstage area. Look for specific items: (a) Where are the different types of microphones and how do they work? (b) How many kinds of lights are there and how are they controlled? What happens if you stand under the lights for some time? (c) Are there moving parts to the stage floor? (d) How are they operated? (e) Are there multiple curtains and backdrops?

5. When you write or adapt your story, you may wish to use a story guide as an aid.

Story Guide

Title

Author

Setting

       Characters (major and secondary)

       Place of action

       Time of action

The problem—what is it? why is it a problem?

The goal—how will the problem be solved?

       Event 1

       Event 2

       Event 3

       and all further events leading to the resolution

The resolution or outcome

The entire class can brainstorm ideas for the episode, but you may wish to break the class into smaller groups with each responsible for one section of the story.

6. Some students may choose the job of writing a preview of the coming program or an article for the newspaper's TV section. Study examples of articles in magazines or newspapers as a model. Sunday papers often have a special section for these reviews. Consult your library media center for back issues.

7. A story board is usually used in TV production. Each scene is sketched out on a large sheet of paper along with the dialogue. Other students may wish to make these guides and put them in proper sequence for use during filming.

8. A teleprompter helps remind performers of their lines during the filming. This can be made with shelf paper rolled onto paper towel tubes placed about two feet apart.

9. In the book, what special effects were used to create the illusions of the superhero and the set itself? What "tricks" will you need for your production? (Think of your favorite superhero programs for clues.) What materials or devices will be needed to carry them out?

10. Music is used for effect. How does it create an image? What kind of music would help show excitement, suspense, terror, happiness, etc.? Select music for your episode of "The Bionic Bunny Show."

11. Watch someone demonstrate the use of makeup, including fake moustaches, wigs, padding, etc., to change the looks of someone. Why do actors and actresses need to wear makeup for both live and filmed performances? How is the makeup applied? What substances must be used to remove it?

12. Have a person explain the operation of a videocamera. Can you see the picture as it is filming? Is the camera hand-held or stationary? How sensitive is the camera microphone to voices and extra sounds in the room? Make some practice tapes so you become comfortable working in front of a camera.

13. What is the difference between making a movie of your production and videotaping it? What do you see if you look at a piece of movie film? Can you examine videotape?

14. Have a dress-up day when students become the bionic hero of their choice.

15. Make commercials advertising your new episode of "The Bionic Bunny Show." Videotape these to evaluate your performance and see how convincing you were.

16. Bionic starts with a prefix "bio-" which means life. What other words start with this prefix? (Do not confuse this with "bi-" which means two.) What does "bionic" mean? Are there bionic devices in existence today?

17. The Bionic Bunny is a superhero. What does this mean to you? What person do you consider to be a superhero? Write about this person—he or she could be famous or someone who shares your life.

18. Do you prefer cartoon superheroes or ones played by real persons? Some animated shows are based on actual people or on other programs which starred actual performers, e.g., "Fat Albert" is based on Bill Cosby's real-life childhood, and "Star Trek" the cartoon show is based on the original series starring William Shatner and Leonard Nimoy. Which show do you prefer? What are the advantages and disadvantages of the cartoon and the real versions? What production processes would be similar or different?

19. Start a fan club for the Bionic Bunny. Design a membership card, Bionic Bunny button, T-shirt and bionic ears. You might also wish to offer posters, key chains, or other objects to members. Make examples of these from art supply scraps or items you can bring into school.

35

BATTERIES AND ELECTRIC CIRCUITS

Dear Mr. Henshaw
Beverly Cleary
New York: Dell, 1983

Summary

When Leigh Botts finds that someone is stealing food from his lunch, he decides to catch the culprit by setting an alarm in his lunch box. His journal carefully details all the steps of the process.

Science Topic Areas

Electric current, batteries, voltage

Content Related Words

Battery, circuit, voltage, volts, amps, watts, insulator

Note: These activities are based on the book's diary entries for Thursday, March 1, through Saturday, March 24. The entire book may be read to the class or the section on batteries may be used separately.

Activities

1. Learn the symbols and diagram of a wiring pattern. (See figure 35.1.)

2. What material is used to insulate wire? Why must this be done? Have someone demonstrate the proper way to cut and strip insulated wire.

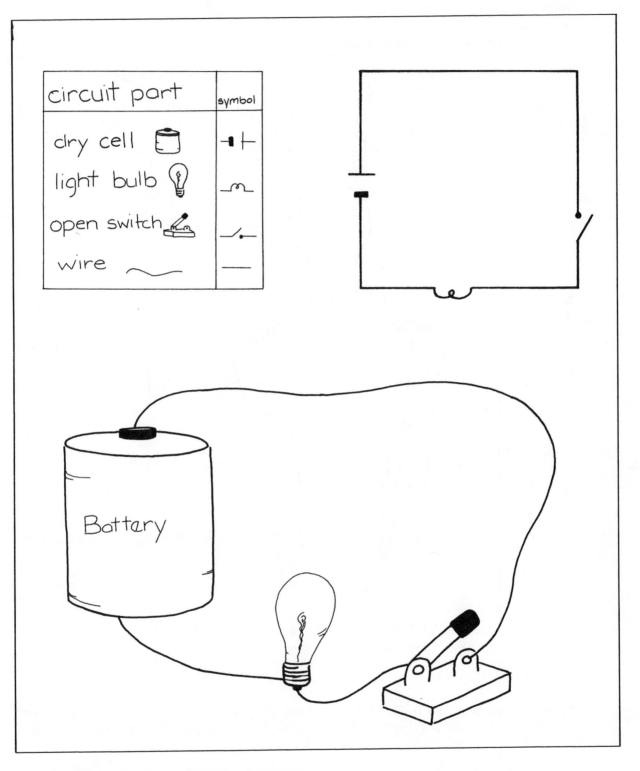

Fig. 35.1. Wiring Pattern, Symbols, and Diagram.

3. Make a battery. (See figure 35.2.)

4. Make a flashlight. (See figure 35.3.)

5. Hook up an alarm to a box as Leigh Botts did (see figure 35.4.). Write up the activity including the materials used and steps of the process. Draw a diagram of the device and make a sequential explanation of the process, from flipping the switch to ringing the buzzer.

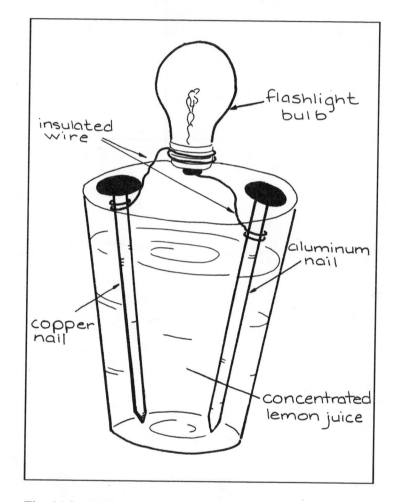

Fig. 35.2. A Homemade Battery.

6. Write a letter to Leigh Botts describing your alarm-in-a-box project. How were your experiences the same or different? Are there things either of you should change if you do this again?

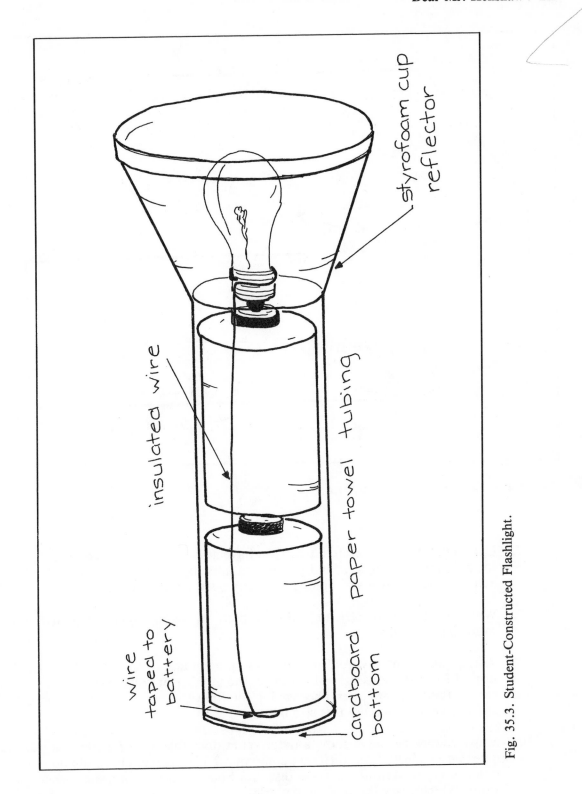

styrofoam cup
reflector

insulated wire

cardboard   paper towel   tubing

wire
taped to
battery

bottom

Fig. 35.3. Student-Constructed Flashlight.

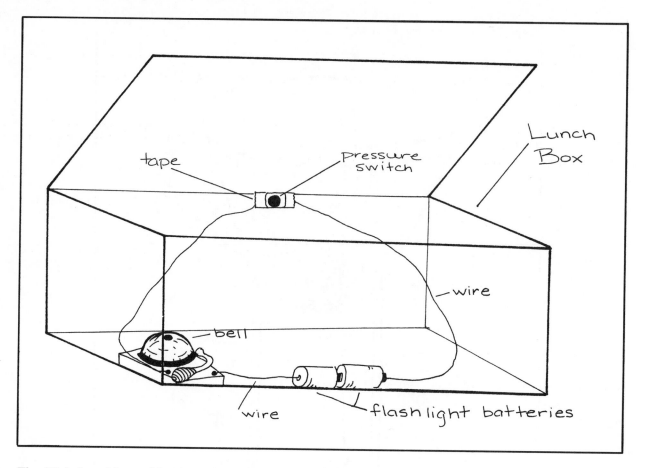

Fig. 35.4. Lunchbox with Alarm System.

7. List all the battery-operated items you have at home. Look in a discount store catalog for additional examples. Find pictures in advertisements and make a display of these items. Label the size and number of batteries they require.

8. What are the advantages and disadvantages of battery-operated items? A chart can show these visually.

9. Visit a battery display in a store or look in a catalog or sale flyer from an electronics store. List the various sizes of batteries, the number of volts they produce, the cost per battery (batteries are often packaged in multiple numbers, so you may need to divide), and the items which use this size battery.

10. Many battery packages show a date. What does this mean? Is there a wide range of dates on products from different companies? If possible, check the date on the same type battery in various stores—a discount house, a drug store, the corner convenience store. Which carry the freshest batteries?

11. Compare the cost and projected life of regular and rechargeable batteries of the same size. Which is a better investment?

12. Automobile batteries are among the largest made. Using a catalog or sale flyer from an auto store or auto department, compare car batteries — size, voltage, cost, guarantee, special features, etc.

13. Read the guarantee from two or three different batteries made by the same company. How are they alike? What features are different? What does the manufacturer promise the customer? What must the customer do? Compare guarantees from different companies.

14. Have someone demonstrate the use of automobile battery cables. In writing, explain their purpose and how they operate.

15. You have been asked to head an advertising campaign for a battery manufacturer. Design a "battery mascot" by using art supply scraps and an old battery. Then make up a slogan or saying which can represent your company and indicate the worth of your product. Have a contest to see who is hired.

Related Books and References

Reuben, Gabriel. *Electricity Experiments for Children*. New York: Dover Publications, 1968.

APPENDIX
SOLUTIONS TO PUZZLES

Answer Keys

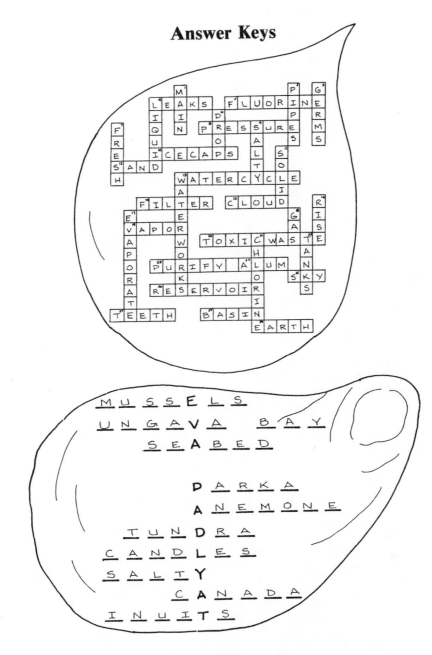

INDEX